A BEAUTIFUL FRIENDSHIP
The Joy of Chasing Bogey Golf

Phil Fitzpatrick

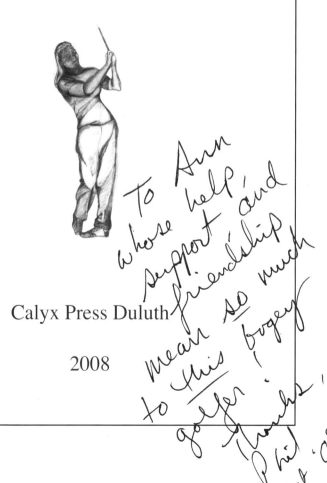

Calyx Press Duluth

2008

To Ann
whose help,
support and
friendship
mean so much
to this bogey
golfer!
Thanks!
Phil
Oct '08

ISBN # 0-9772376-8-0

Introduction

> Golf is deceptively simple,
> endlessly complicated. A child
> can play it well and a grown
> man can never master it. It
> is almost a science, yet it is a
> puzzle with no answer.
>
> > Arnold Palmer

> Golf is twenty percent mechanics
> and technique. The other eighty
> percent is philosophy, humor,
> tragedy, romance, melodrama,
> companionship, camaraderie,
> cussedness, and conversation.
>
> > Grantland Rice

Virtually any golfer could write a book like this, even you, but I thought I'd save you the trouble. Then, too, I'd hate for you to miss the kind of sleep I missed while trying to find just the right thing to say to a wide range of devotees, diehards, and dreamers, even though there *is* a definite high that you get from late night (or early morning) writing—especially when you're excited by the topic. And that's me; I am currently entering the fifth season of being buzzed about this topic. Empirical evidence gathered from club houses, scrambles, sitting in front of televised tournaments, and practice sessions tells me that I am not alone. A book about the joy of chasing bogey golf is long overdue.

I'm what might be termed a casual golfer. I play three or four times a week in the summer, fewer in the spring and fall. Given the winters here in Duluth, Minnesota, my clubs go unused from about mid-October to mid-April—if I'm lucky. (I am editing this manuscript on April 13th, and there are still eight inches of snow on the ground!) Even so, I play in one of the best locations in the Upper Midwest. Although the courses are open for only about six months, there are many holes on several of our courses where, beyond the fairways and greens, a golfer can look out to the immense blue-grey eye of Lake Superior. Of course, that privilege is far from the only reason that I've come to love this game, and you will find few references to lake views herein, but it is a very real and significant part of a seven-year love affair that has culminated in this book. Play just one round with a good friend here in Duluth on the Lakes Nine at Lester Park Golf Course on a sunny weekday morning in June, for instance, and you'll see what I mean. Better yet, go play a round with an ideal playing partner on a favorite course anywhere, keeping just a few of the ideas you find in this book in mind, and you'll see what I mean; my course, inspiring and beautiful as it is, doesn't have a monopoly on beautiful vistas. I know that many of you understand implicitly what I mean.

From the title of this book, you might conclude that not only am I encouraging you to be more realistic about your golf game, but actually to adopt—right from the start—a defeatist attitude about playing the game. You might then justifiably suggest that I take a more positive attitude. You might, in fact, wonder why the book is not titled *Five Secrets to Playing **Par** Golf* or even just *Five Secrets to Playing **Better** Golf*. These could be interesting books in their own right, and many such books are available, but I have a specific purpose in mind for this book.

As casual golfers, we would all love to have a handicap of zero; aiming to be a scratch golfer is not necessarily all that distasteful or preposterous an ambition. This is true especially if you have a good combination of time, motivation, and money for greens fees, lessons, and golf junkets on your hands.

There can be no denying that par should be every golfer's ambition, and I don't intend to settle for bogey golf if and when I finally can achieve par consistently. I suspect that many of you reading this book are playing better than bogey golf already, but I hope that at least a few of the ideas, perspectives, experiences, and theories I offer will help no matter what your handicap is. Actually, I want to extend that hope to include your playing partners, your children, and even those in your life who do not yet play golf but who might one day be inspired by your delight in the sport to take it up. I trust that I am not overly idealistic and naïve in hoping that the book offers a little something for everyone.

The unvarnished truth is that I have been looking for an excuse to write a book about golf ever since I started playing, even though when I look over the "Golf" section in bookstores, I wonder why anyone in his or her right mind would bother. The market is glutted. There are coffee table books, biographies and autobiographies, and plenty of instructional books to name just a few. In other words, you name the genre, and there are scores of books to represent it. Most of my ruminations about writing a book on golf, therefore, had been short-lived and unrealistic—until a sunny October day in 2004.

I had just played my final round of the season that day. Like a misty genie hissing forth from an antique bottle, the idea for the book emerged full-blown at two thirty in the morning. I was trying to reclaim just enough of the blankets hogged by my black lab, Leo, to cover my shoulders and protect me from the autumn breezes riffling through the open window. These were the remnants of strong winds that had swirled around my playing partner and me the afternoon before.

It was a round we almost didn't play, but I am sure that some unseen power moved us mysteriously but firmly from saying in the comfort of our own living rooms, "It's too windy," to a far more elevated and inspired state of mind and body after an absolutely wondrous nine holes of autumn golf. We both agreed that it was the best round the two of us had played all season. The hidden force that got us out there that day must have been the same one that prompted me not to give up on a lofty drive I had sliced off the tee on the final hole but, instead, to look for it—and find it—just inside the edge of the cart path far below.

I'm also certain that it is the very same power that has kept me thinking excitedly, if gingerly, about the idea for this book ever since, the same power that gives me the sense to set my sights on very realistic goals each time I go out to play golf. But I'm getting ahead of myself.

The other seminal idea for this book came from a man about my age whom I'd never met before and have not seen since. After we played nine holes together as total strangers and had conversed casually about how enjoyable the game is, especially when you don't expect miracles every time you address the ball, I asked him a simple question: "If you could read a book on golf, any book that is still unwritten, what kind of a book would it be?" He answered quickly, and with some degree of self-assurance, that the most useful book for a golfer at our level would be a book about how to do your best given your own limitations, about how to enjoy the game despite having a handicap of, say, 20, and about how to improve certain aspects of your game without necessarily having to take countless lessons or go to Qualifying School to do it.

I understood immediately. I filled in the "bogey golf" idea shortly after that conversation. This book's raison d'etre, then, the quality that makes it unique among the other books next to it on the "Golf" shelf at your local bookstore, is that what it touts as desirable and quite attainable is the very thing most golfers automatically think of as undesirable: shooting bogey.

Before continuing, please keep three things in mind: First, I am righthanded, so when I refer to thumbs or elbows or the way you are facing, assume that I mean it as a right-handed golfer. If you're a lefty, make sure to switch all the references to the other side.

Second, my partner and I play the white (intermediate) tees, so on the rare occasions when I refer to distances and yardage, assume we tee off from the white tees.

Third, I refer to that playing partner frequently, so I use the abbreviation "IPP" to mean "ideal playing partner." Few golfers are lucky enough to have one, but a little looking, coupled with a little risk taking, and you never know who you might find. Perhaps you already have one. If so, you have probably discovered how the companionship takes your game to a whole different level.

I hope you enjoy this book. It is written so you may dive in at any place and read for as long or short a period of time as you want. Pick your favorite chapters, dogear them, quote from them at will, memorize some of the quotes. I hope it helps you enjoy the game of golf a little bit more. I also hope you can find the time, the inspiration, and the audience to write your own book some day. Writing about golf is almost as much fun as playing it…almost.

CHAPTER ONE
EMBRACING BOGEY

You can't always get what you want
But if you try sometimes you might find
You get what you need.

The Rolling Stones

It's not just what you're given,
It's what you do with what you've got.

Si Kahn

History

Having realized a few years ago that I was a little too long in the tooth even to dream of making the PGA Tour, I looked for the next best thing. I did not want to say, "I'm a scratch golfer," or "My handicap is under double digits." I couldn't really be "tournament ready," "applying to Qualifying School," or even "club champion." I wanted nothing more than to be able to say, "I play bogey golf."

I like the name "bogey." The word has muscle and swagger. Each time I address the ball, I hear echoes of Humphrey Bogart in the film *Casablanca* saying, "Here's looking at you, Kid." I want to be the guy who's always got that "We'll always have Paris" look about him whether I'm on the tee, on the green, or in the woods. (In which case, it would be, "Here's looking *for* you, Kid.") It wouldn't matter where I was, though: in the fairway, in the rough, or in a more disconcerting spot. It wouldn't matter because I could get out of the tight spot—not with my three wood nor by hitting a ball lying up against the wrong side of a tree, left-handed. No, it would be because I could shift the cigarette butt over to the other side of my lips, roll up my sleeves, peer condescendingly down through the woods at the flag, take one practice swing, barely clip the top of the dirt with my four iron, deftly lift the ball from its buried lie, and send it over the creek, between two oak trunks, and out onto the fairway, just below the green for an easy up-and-down.

Not, mind you, to save par, but to save...*bogey!*

Bogey: one stroke over par. Very simple to understand, but not very simple to achieve.

It is simple enough to understand especially for those of us who do not get exemptions to tournaments, monogrammed ball caps, or commercial endorsements—unless they be from someone whom we might have left at home, who, anticipating an afternoon alone, yells out the endorsement, "Go get em, Tiger! Have fun!" and does so, presumably, with a wry, unseen smile. "Fun" isn't always connected with the pursuit of bogey golf, but with the right perspective, it *can* be. When I stopped thinking of my three wood as a millstone or an albatross and started thinking of it as Excalibur, Wonderboy, or Lucille, I began having more fun. "Have fun" for me translates to a number of things once I'm on the course, and playing bogey golf is now my Holy Grail. It is at the heart of my approach to this crazy, mysterious, lovable game.

When my ideal playing partner (IPP) steps up to the first tee and goes through his warm-ups and practice swings, he almost always says, "Let's have fun, Fitz!" It sounds optimistic and rejuvenating, a positive way to begin the round, a sort of

"Pick yourself up, dust yourself off, and start all over again" exhortation. I usually counter with the more stoical "We'll give it our best shot," or perhaps I'll mumble the resolute "Yep!" when I'm feeling a little more on the monosyllabic side. Once in a great while, if I've had my orange juice and it's a bright Saturday morning and I have honors and we're not going to be pressed from behind, I'll say "That's just what I aim to do, Pal!" That's when I feel like bogey golf is somewhere within striking distance.

No matter how many mulligans it takes us to get off the first tee on those rare days, trying to scramble my way to a 45 for nine holes will not just be tilting at windmills. I won't be Don Quixote, Walter Mitty, or even the very nonfictional F. Scott Fitzgerald full of a naïve faith in the infinite possibilities that lie ahead. I would be a little more along the lines of Tattered Tom or Ragged Dick, characters from the 19th-century Horatio Alger novels: a little down on my luck with a few too many obstacles standing in my way, but with a strong sense that giving it "the old college try" might just be enough. Playing bogey golf is not quite the same as rising from the ash heap like the Phoenix. Succeeding at playing bogey golf isn't really a "Eureka!" moment, either, because that suggests a miracle discovery. Playing bogey golf is more like we're setting up base camp in the foothills and securing a reliable supply position; we're content to remain in the safe zone while the sherpas and the technicians (the pros, the naturals, and the scratch golfers) climb through the brisk clouds trying to reach the rarified air of the mountaintop that is par.

The term "bogey" originated across the Atlantic in the late 19th century; it had something to do with a mythical standard number of strokes that golfers would try to match or outdo. The term "par" had not yet arrived on the scene, so quite paradoxically, bogey was actually par. It was not until the early 20th-century, when the classier, more desirable and elevated word "par" was co-opted from the business world, that the word "bogey" was relegated to the ranks of "bridesmaid," "second fiddle," or, dare we say, "loser"? Bogey, now the equivalent of one stroke *over* par, gradually but inexorably became the sort of red ribbon of golf, a score that gets an ugly box around it while a birdie (one stroke *under* par) gets a perfect circle around it on tournament scorecards.

I prefer, however, to give the word "bogey" its rightful place in the hierarchy of golf terms. It has an honorable place in my game because I understand its history. I like its associations with the 1930s and 1940s when hard work and pluck and learning how to do without became not just fashionable but necessary and collaborative. Now that I've done it once or twice, I know that bogey is an achievable goal for me; it feels like a gutsy, lunch pail sort of "slugging it out in the trenches" status symbol especially for someone who is just slightly past peak and who usually needs any old port in a storm out on the golf course.

Though there is definitely something I like about the word "bogey" to the point where I've developed a fondness for the term, I certainly make no pretensions about not caring whether I ever shoot par. That objective is always a given—for any golfer. But par requires a little bit of luck in addition to more than a little bit of skill. This latter commodity seems to be in rather short supply, so, as Mark Twain says of Truth, "Let us economize it!" I'll always take a par when it comes, and there have been rounds when I have come close to actually having more pars than bogeys on my scorecard. I cannot afford, however, to make shooting par a significant component of my strategic plan when I'm playing a round of golf. There are veteran professionals playing on the PGA tour as you read this whose strategic plan is very much about par and who regularly crash and burn in their season long attempts to reach it. No, I know myself well enough not to spend time, energy, and money on what can be little more than a fantasy.

Par *would* evoke a "Eureka!" response in me, but not because I have totally given up on the possibility. It's simply a matter of not putting much stock in something that happens so infrequently. I can tell you just how often it happens, in fact, because I play about one hundred rounds each summer and shoot par on maybe a dozen holes. So, let's say, generously, twenty pars over 1,500 holes. You do the math; I'm too embarrassed.

People look at me strangely when I say that I am serious about accepting bogey as par. I don't think it's that big a deal, but there is a popular and very American notion that bogey equals second best, and who in his or her right mind would publicly state that settling for second best is just fine? I can read their minds just by looking in their eyes and paying attention to their body language: "If you settle for bogey, you'll never reach par!" Maybe so, but that is not so bad. Really. I hope this book will dispel some of the myths surrounding the purgatory, the ignominy that is supposed to accompany settling for second best. It starts with being able to understand and live with one's limitations. In other words, it starts with redefining "limitations" to mean "capabilities."

Here's an example: I know I cannot hit a 300-yard drive unless there's a strong tailwind, unless the fairway slopes downhill precipitously toward the green, and unless I hit my drive straight. The first two conditions occur much more frequently than the third. I'm not getting any younger or stronger, either. The 200-yard drive is hard enough, but the 300-yard drive is just plain unrealistic. Here's how I choose to view that fact, however: I don't *need* a 300-yard drive *if* I can put together the rest of my game well enough. So I'm just trying to work on straightness, or at least reducing the arc on my slices (see Chapter 9). I would rather have a straight 200-yarder than a sliced or hooked 300-yarder. For me, straightness is *way* more satisfying. Actually, *control* is more satisfying. Straightness and accuracy are a by-product of control. I'm distinguishing here between the "control" that men and women argue about when deciding who's in charge of the grocery shopping, balancing the checkbook, or disciplining the kids. I'm hardly a control freak at home or in the classroom or with friends, but on the golf course, I've decided that I can aspire to being a control freak. Having said this, it's very important to distinguish between the control I have a few seconds *before* striking the ball, and the control of the ball's flight path a few seconds *after* striking it. If playing bogey golf is going to happen, it will happen because I am mastering the former and letting go of the latter. It's about process, not product.

I like par, and my partner and I praise ourselves and each other when we achieve it, but quite frankly, I'm getting deeper into believing that chasing bogey makes sense. If you're into pars and *only* pars, maybe this isn't the book for you. But perhaps you're fooling yourself and enjoying golf less than you might, and this *is* just the book for you.

Reality

Playing bogey golf consistently requires many sacrifices. Beer, donuts, fast food, fairway woods in the deep rough, sleeping in, atheism—these have to go. You cannot hope to play bogey golf without giving up some indulgences and some excesses. I don't include swearing on this list, but that may be coming soon, maybe by the time you're reading this book. Above all, you have to give up two things: You have to give up not caring, and you have to give up caring too much.

What does that mean? It means that you *might* just have to adopt The Way of Zen. I can well remember a number of moments when The Way of Zen seemed like my only option. This "way" or "path" has much to offer, but it doesn't work if you take it lightly. You have to be willing to commit, and you can't be a two-timer, a flake, a fair-weather friend, or an "I'm the boss of me" kind of rebel. Let me emphasize that The Way of Zen isn't *the* answer, it is only *an* answer.

Here's how to buy into The Way of Zen: Do it the night before, or the day before, or the winter before your next round—*not* after you've snap-hooked three or four balls into the pond left of the fairway on the second hole at Lester Park Golf Course in Duluth, Minnesota and sent flocks of geese into the air. You can't adopt it after three of your best putts have lipped out, nor after you've double-bogeyed all the par 3s on the course. You have to phase it in gradually and consistently rather than trying to shift into it in high gear when the wheels are coming off the wagon. For The Way of Zen to work for you, here are three pieces of advice:

1. Read up on it.
2. Believe in it wholeheartedly.
3. Practice it.

I could say the same thing, of course, about your swing, your stance, your follow-through, or your putting. Zen and bogey golf fit pretty well together, but they both require your undivided attention, your unfailing commitment, and *your* word against all detractors. They also demand the patience of Job. So when you want to build a small golf library for yourself, start with the *Bible* and the *Tao Te Ching* (see Chapter 6). I have flirted with bogey golf going on three years now. That's long enough to know that—absolutely—I am ready to embrace consistent bogey golf. I aim to have it become my standard—just like it was for those fellows across the Atlantic back in the 1890s. To "settle" for bogey golf is too pejorative and resigned an approach. That sounds like "I will content myself with … " or "I will accept … " or "I'll be happy if I *only* play bogey golf." It's not that at all, for there's a fine line between playing bogey golf consistently and being happy with that, and entering into the competitive, agitated, nerve-wracking world of playing par golf consistently. The former I now occasionally manage, and I hope to master it before another year or so goes by. The latter I will never be able to reach—not in this life, anyway. At present, though, the good news is that I am beginning to know the difference.

CHAPTER TWO
MINDFULNESS AND THE DOCTRINE OF "LESS IS MORE"

You must live in the present,
launch yourself on every wave,
find your eternity in each
moment.

        Henry David Thoreau

I'd play every day if I could. It's
cheaper than a shrink and there
are no telephones on my golf
cart.

        Brent Musburger

In my idyllic childhood, when I would run the lawn mower through a patch of poison ivy, or cross my skis doing a snowplow during a ski lesson, or take my eyes off the road while driving the family car, my father, in a noticeably exasperated tone of voice, would bark out,

Philip, you've got to keep your wits about you!

Forty-five years later, I know that in this terse hybrid of Depression Era and World War II thinking, he was talking about *mindfulness*—another of the growing list of character traits we "Sensitive New Age Guys" have added to our resumes over the last twenty years. I know Dad wouldn't have chosen to use that word even if he had known it at the time. It's too New Age-y, and he was anything but a New Age-type guy. He was old school, a member of what Tom Brokaw refers to as "The Greatest Generation"—World War II veteran, mountain climber, lumberjack, downhill racer, a bootstrap man who didn't have time for pat phrases, psychobabble, narcissism—much less the kind of deliberate reflection I recommend in this book. It was all about keeping your mind on your work, getting the job done and done well, and not expecting any fanfare or thanks along the way. Nonetheless, it was mindfulness he was trying to sell me on; he himself practiced it to a fault.

I wish I had known then what I know now about keeping my wits about me. Maybe I would have earned a bit more approval from Dad—but that's a "whole nuther story." I certainly would have had fewer unforced errors on the tennis court, fewer stitches, fewer car accidents, and fewer C-minuses. I still have trouble with mindfulness; I leave my wedge at the side of the green at least three or four times a summer. When it comes right down to it, just like anything else, golf is about little else than mindfulness—from tee to green; this is especially so when we play for some of its more subtle and enchanting aspects rather than just for a lower score.

Mindfulness has a curious quality about it that almost defies articulation. When it first occurred to me to do a chapter on this topic, I really struggled with just how to approach it because you cannot really grit your teeth, roll up your sleeves, bear down—and be mindful. It has to become a part of you in the same way that breathing or walking does—but we do these more or less without thinking. There is a curious dualism about mindfulness; it implies both responsiveness and unresponsiveness. To put it in other words, mindfulness must effectively be the opposite of itself in the sense that mindful people are so attuned to their surroundings that their minds, the thinking and planning and organizing and deciding parts, become not inactive or dormant but utterly patient, receptive, and still.

In Chapter 6, I recommend reading a famous letter by English poet John Keats about what he calls "Negative Capability." When you locate the letter and read it, you may understand what I am suggesting: namely, that in golf, as elsewhere in life, "less is more." Here is a fragment of that letter written on December 21, 1817 to Keats's brothers George and Thomas that might put mindfulness into a softer, more delicate light:

> ... *The excellence of every Art is*
> *its intensity, capable of making all*
> *disagreeables evaporate, from their*
> *being in close relationship with*
> *Beauty & Truth—Examine King*
> *Lear & you will find this exemplified*
> *throughout; but in this picture we*
> *have unpleasantness without any*
> *momentous depth of speculation*
> *excited, in which to bury its*
> *repulsiveness—The picture is larger*
> *than Christ rejected—it struck me,*
> *what quality which Shakespeare*
> *possessed so enormously—I*
> *mean Negative Capability, that is*
> *when man is capable of being in*
> *uncertainties, Mysteries, doubts,*
> *without any irritable reaching after*
> *fact & reason ...*

This is pretty heady stuff for a golf book, yes, but please don't let it put you off. Read it again, and focus on the final few lines. Though I admire Keats—and Shakespeare even more—I will leave the pursuit of these two sages and their own exquisite and compelling mindfulness for another time. My point is that, like baseball, another sport in which time is unimportant while grass is, and where the flight of a ball can be viewed both as purposeful *and* aesthetically pleasing, golf benefits from certain connections to literature. The above fragment contains a few seeds that surely did not originate for Keats in any golf-related context, but they may well be relevant to pursuing a score that is satisfying even though it is a bit less than perfect, a bit more than par.

First, attend to Keats's phrase, "capable of being in uncertainties." Now, think about its opposite. I can imagine you replying in an argumentative tone of voice,

> *Certainty is what I live for, and that's what I want in my golf game!*

I understand, and I feel your pain. I, too, need certainty. But where my golf game is concerned, I have neither the time, nor the money, nor the inclination to work diligently enough to get good enough to be certain of the outcome on every one of my shots. If you do have that kind of time, count your blessings. Why are you reading this book? Get out there and protect your precious little certainty. The rest of us shirt-sleeve types are going to have to embrace its opposite just to survive, let alone succeed. Keats is onto something very helpful here without his ever having picked up a golf club. It has something to do with how crucial it is **to understand the hazards of certainty**, the hazard of believing we know for sure what a particular outcome will be. Unorthodox though it may sound, considering how much we like just to *know* something, Keats is arguing in favor not only of *not* knowing everything but of being comfortable in, and actually valuing, that kind of "not knowing."

Mindfulness and the Doctrine of "Less Is More"

Before I lose you, we need to get out on the golf course. You must be wondering what all this "being comfortable not knowing" has to do with mindfulness, let alone with scoring bogey. Wouldn't it seem that keeping your wits about you (being mindful) would be quite the opposite of being comfortable with "uncertainty"? Mindfulness is being completely tuned in to the things that make up the present moment. If that's so, how can I also be "capable of being in uncertainties"? What uncertainties can there be when one is mindful? Work with me on this: when my mind is alert and clear, I know things, I am not burdened with doubt or confusion, and I am focused.

Suppose you're looking at your nicely positioned drive out there in the middle of the fairway some 200 yards or so off the tee. It's a straightforward 400-yard par 4, much like our first hole on the front nine here at Lester Park, with few hazards or bunkers. This is a hole, in other words, quite common at local public golf courses and quite uncommon at Augusta National, Pebble Beach, or Carnoustie. It's a hole with a fairly sizeable margin for error: an absence of hazards, a wide fairway, and the chance for a solid first shot. What's left not to be certain about? Consider the possibility that there is more uncertainty than meets the eye. You may not know which club to use.

In order to solve that issue, you have to think about how to factor in the gentle incline up to the green. After that, you'll want to consider how well or poorly you're hitting your fairway woods lately. And after that, if you choose to go with an iron, and you've picked out your four iron because it's uphill, you'll be thinking about how much muscle you must put into the shot.

No matter how many of these questions you resolve quickly and confidently in your mind, there are going to be some variables in the shot, right? We try to keep the variables as few and as manageable as possible when we play, but we can't eliminate them altogether. So, our own shots are generally better when we assume a certain amount of *variability* despite putting our absolute best effort into them. The reason for this is simple: accepting a certain degree of lack of control over any given shot removes, at least for the moment, any compulsiveness about those variables that will interfere with the mechanics of the shot and disrupt the flow. When a ladybug lands on your ball just as you are about to putt, a tiny bit of certainty disappears, unless you incorporate the bug into the process. Mindfulness incorporates variability into a present and totally engaged state of being. Mindfulness allows chance to play a role.

Think about your swing for a moment. Let's hope that it has evolved to the point where it is relatively familiar, comfortable, and practiced enough so that every new swing is more or less the same as the last one. That's the key for every serious or even half-serious golfer—to have a *repeatable* swing. Being mindful about the swing is going to maximize the chance that it will be a fairly good copy of its predecessors. Allowing yourself to rest easy about the uncertainty of the moment allows for some slight variations without those wheels coming off the wagon.

If your swing works for you, that's about the best thing you can say about your game. But it's far from perfect, and right there is the uncertainty. Accept it, and you will worry less, and with less worry comes more mindfulness. Less perfection, more comfort. Less distress about outcome, more delight in the process. Less preoccupation with certainty, and more ability to maximize potential within the bounds of uncertainty.

Let me provide a little more "grounding" in the real world of the golf course by revisiting some of my own experiences. I recall many times when I was having difficulty, when I felt I needed some sort of steadying idea or focal point to help me "regroup" and get me out of a negative mind set. It's always a bit ironic to be playing a game we love and somehow finding ourselves in a foul humor while playing. Such an inherently satisfying game, so unsatisfying a performance, I mean. There are two things I do when this happens:

I check my grip
I remind myself that gripping a club is not a matter of the proverbial "choke hold" or "white knuckle grab." The club must be gripped securely, but I am stopping short of using the word "firmly" here. Gripping your club too tightly can result in many undesirable things, such as too rushed a swing, digging the blade into the turf, a slice, excess body movement, increased tension and jerkiness, or all of the above. A golf swing, for all its explosiveness at impact, is the gentle act of creating a flight that, for purely aesthetic pleasure in sports, simply has no parallel. You don't have to hold on for dear life when gripping your club, so check it when things aren't going well for you. Take plenty of practice swings, and feel the club *nestled in* your hands rather than *gripped by* them. Listen to the legendary Sam Snead's perfect metaphor for what a golf grip should be: "Hold the club like you are holding a baby bird."

I try hard not to try too hard
This second tip is much less technical, and failure to keep it in mind as much as anything

causes the grip problem above. Mindfulness can keep you from trying too hard on the course. After inadequate preparation or injury, trying too hard or "pressing" is an athlete's worst enemy. Here is where the "less is more" slogan must come into play. Mindfulness will help you to stay calm and relaxed in the midst of concentration, but the concentration itself must be about the process, not about the product. In other words, thinking too much about "killing it," or about hitting the best shot of your life, or recovering all at once from a bad hole, are all thoughts about product, about objective, about outcome. Less thinking will produce, *most of the time*, more satisfaction and success eventually. Trying too hard often results in horrible shots. One of the best examples of this is when you hit a carbon copy of a really bad shot after you have resolved with a grimace that you will hit it right the second time. I have lost count of the number of times my IPP and I have hit pairs of equally disastrous shots to our great embarrassment and shame—and wonder. How can such a thing happen? I don't ever hope to understand exactly how it can, but I'd be surprised if it hasn't happened to you. I only know that it in quite a mysterious way it is connected with trying too hard.

If I were to make a list here, I'd do it using the word "less" at the beginning of each one, and list the positive things that occur when I stop trying too hard. I'd start with "less tension" and continue through "less inept shots" (that should be *fewer* inept shots, but you get the idea), and "less anxiety." Normally, if I can put "trying too hard" behind me for a whole round, I wind up with *fewer* shots, too. I always play better when I am more mindful of the day and its beauty than about whether I'm in the lead or behind, whether I might still break 50 for nine holes, whether or not my swing looks professional.

If I accept Keats's "uncertainties, Mysteries, doubts" that are built into the game and my state of mind, I wind up enjoying the round much more. Usually I play better, too. There have been days when the pleasure of seeing my IPP conquer a particular par 3 that consistently gives him trouble ended up being the highlight of the day. I love the feel of a nine iron in my hand on that same exact hole and imagining the flight of the ball even before I put my tee in the ground. I try hard to remember on that hole more than most other par 3s to "let the club do the work." In a sort of Yogi Berra-type way, I am trying hard not to try too hard.

One final word about buying into the idea that "less is more": if you change "less" to "fewer," then the phrase is also quite relevant to the topic of scoring. The object of the game is fewer shots. But keeping with the word "less," and leaving the scoring to take care of itself, think about "less" when it comes to club choice. I *still* get confused by the relationship between "too much club" or "not enough club" and the number on the club head, but I think I have finally figured it out, and this is how it goes: the higher the number, the more loft there will be on the shot, and so, the lower the distance—or the shorter the shot. If someone tells you that you had "too much club" on your shot, he means you used a club whose number was too low. This means, in other words, that the angle of the club face was too small. Get it? Too much club = too low a number = too small an angle = too much distance and not enough loft.

For example, if you hit a seven iron from one hundred yards out and fly the green, then you either don't know your own strength, or you chose a club whose number is too low (whose angle is too small) for the shot. Maybe an eight iron, in this example, would have been a better choice. I've always felt that for us would-be bogey golfers, it's wiser to come up a bit short than it is to shoot way past your intended target. So, "less is more" might apply to being somewhat conservative in your club choice until you know your own strength well enough to choose a lower rather than a higher numbered club.

To push this just a bit further, "less is more" will be translated as "more is less" if you'd rather risk being a bit short of your target than have your shot land beyond your target. To put it more simply, a higher numbered club will yield a shorter distance on the shot because the club gives the ball more loft and less distance due to the greater angle of the club face. More (club number and club angle) yields less (distance), in short.

Be mindful of your clubs and your strength and your swing as your game progresses, and discover how "less is more" can have quite a wide spectrum of meanings for you during a round. Mindfulness has both very specific and very broad implications in the game of golf, and discovering how it relates to your golf game as well as your life is part of the pleasure of becoming more intimately involved with the quest to play bogey golf.

CHAPTER THREE
CLUBS ARE TRUMP

Someone once asked me what my
favorite club was. I said, "All of
them."

> Tiger Woods

If a lot of people gripped a knife and
fork the way they do a golf club,
they'd starve to death.

> Sam Snead

I love my clubs. Got 'em at Play It Again Sports. A hundred
bucks and change. Strategy Model 121 Nickel Stainless. I've
had them for six summers now, and I can't imagine ever
exchanging them for another set, though I suppose I will some
day soon. It will be a rough day when I have to change; these
clubs have seen me through many memorable moments. They
seem like trusted friends now, and believe me, they behave
just like friends! If I treat them with respect, let them be who
they are, keep them in the loop with me, allow them their own
individuality, let them do the work, give them time off for
good behavior when they deserve it, and avoid clutching them
too tightly, they repay me constantly and generously.

I'd like to comment on three of these clubs. I hope doing so
will inspire you to appreciate a few special clubs of your
own even more. Having a favorite club or two can be very
pleasurable, though frustration potential never goes away
completely, for clubs are like fallible human beings. They each
have their limitations, and though each one demands a certain

quality in the way I relate to them, it is very relaxing and reassuring to have them with me on every hole I play.

The Three Wood

I've had this love/hate thing going with fairway woods for a long time; it's only been in recent summers that I've finally developed a lasting and fulfilling relationship with the three wood. When I first began playing seriously, I was petrified at the prospect of using a fairway wood because I thought I always needed a tee for a wood shot. What a rookie! It was an unmitigated disaster every time I'd hit a three wood or a five wood, so for at least two seasons I just left the fairway woods in the bag and used long irons. I could feel the fear mounting if I started to take a fairway wood out of the bag, so I resisted, but I always sensed that I was missing out on something. Finally, I just decided it was time to bite the bullet, and it wasn't long before I discovered how satisfying golf can be when you know how to hit a fairway wood—without a tee. It was glorious! The only thing you have to remember is that whole head thing (see Chapter 7). That's almost the only secret you need to possess in order to have a fighting chance of being successful with fairway woods.

Fairway woods have this mystique about them. They're so tempting to casual golfers in their sleek strength, their promise of distance, of compensating for weak drives and getting us back in the hunt. They're seductive. They seem to dare us to try to exploit their capabilities and experience the thrill of not one but two successive really long shots on any given 400-yard-plus hole. It's that seductiveness that both lured and repelled me for several summers before I finally took the plunge. But before I continue, I owe you some history.

I've completed eight summers of what I'm calling serious golf, although there are as many definitions of that term as there are players. For me, "serious golf" started when my IPP and I needed regular time together to talk leisurely about the softball team we were coaching together. That first summer we must have played at least a couple of rounds per week, and I cannot for the life of me recall how I managed to get through it. I had no skill, no technique, no experience, and no equipment. In addition to that, we usually played the hardest nine hole course in Duluth, the Lakes Nine at Lester Park Golf Course. This course routinely swallows up nearly half a dozen golf balls per golfer per round. It's a narrow, hilly, wooded course with breathtaking views of Lake Superior—and ball-engulfing thickets of pine, poplar, birch, and cottonwood on both sides of all nine fairways. We played this course because it gave us the privacy we wanted. In fact, there were moments when we almost felt claustrophobic in a couple of the narrow fairways, and we were rarely pressed from behind. We always enjoyed the feeling that being so close to Lake Superior would, in a very real sense, elevate both our spirits and our golf games.

Playing the Lakes Nine that summer became a ritual for us. We rarely kept score which was to my advantage because my IPP had been playing for many years. I hasten to add, however, that it was not long before we began sharing perspectives on the topography, terrain, layout, and natural history of this third course at Lester, and also on how to play the course. Having a much stronger drive off the tee than I did at the time, my friend would occasionally announce "Fitz, I'm going for it," on the third hole, a 350-yard hole with a virtual ninety-degree dogleg to the right at the top of a steep uphill slope. There are four bunkers at the top right of the slope. They lurk like sandy versions of Charybdis, the watery vortex Odysseus had to sail past on his way home from the Trojan War. Their entire purpose is to wait, ever ready and ever eager to suck down our drives. To this day, they dare us to try for the languid fairway and gentle approach to the green just over the rise behind them, by shaving the wooded boundary or even by flying over the treetops, tantalized by the prospect neither of bogey nor par, but of birdie. Hearing my partner's proclamation, I'd back up a step or two to watch his ball fly off the tee, ascend rapidly, and do one of three things: 1) slice deep into the trees, 2) fall just short and bounce around and dribble or skip into one of the sand traps, or 3) skim neatly just above the tree line, and on rare occasions, disappear completely from view to drop somewhere just past the peninsula of hardwoods and come to rest within an easy seven iron's reach of the green.

My drive, of course, rarely if ever came anywhere near the top of the hill, and since I had a wicked slice, I'd have to aim way left and risk hitting the gravel cart path that ran along the left-hand side of the fairway at the edge of the woods. If you're getting the sense of a narrow corridor here, fairway bounded on both sides by tall trees, that is correct … and it is typical of the Lakes Nine. No fewer than six of the holes on this course require drives off the tee characterized neither by hook nor slice in order to afford a decent second shot. It was on the widest of one of these six holes, the second, that I began experimenting with my three wood. The second hole is also bounded on both sides by woods, but its straight and relatively flat fairway stretches for nearly 400 yards before swooping up to an elevated green 516 yards from the tee. The fairway gives the impression of forgiveness and invitation, of yawning distance where two good wood shots, at least, are needed to come anywhere close to getting on the green in regulation. Of some significance, too, is the width of the fairway—nearly fifty yards—that provides unusually ample room for error.

I've heard it said that the fairway woods should rarely, if ever, be used to get out of the rough, but a couple of my most memorable three wood shots were out of the deep rough. If I have managed a decent drive off the tee on a par 4 or a par 5, I am often hopeful, maybe even confident, that the three wood can get me almost to the green in regulation if I hit it well. When I practice on the driving range, I can sometimes nearly match the distance I get with my driver with what I get with a good three wood shot. "Sometimes" should actually be "on occasion" or, more accurately, "rarely." The pros use the three wood to contend with a sharp dogleg too near the tee box, or an exceptionally narrow corridor down the first three hundred yards, but I still find that the three wood shots slice just as wickedly as a drive if you aren't careful (see Chapter 9). For bogey golfers, the whole question about using a wood in the rough comes down to two things: how deeply buried in the grass the ball is, and, assuming you hit it well, how clear a shot you have. You have to know your game well enough to be able to answer these two questions almost automatically. As soon as you start "playing Hamlet" (i.e. unable to make up your mind) over one or both of these questions, you need to shift instantaneously to the "safety first" strategy: you cut your losses and head straight back to the fairway without even a thought of advancing the ball. Bottom line: don't be afraid to use your fairway woods. The sooner you make one after another your allies, the sooner your game and your confidence both will improve.

My most glorious and memorable and satisfying three wood outta-the-rough shot was in a member-guest tournament in June 2006 in Ithaca, New York. I was playing with my brother, John, who is six years younger than I am and six strokes better on most days. I remember the ball as being about two hundred yards or so down the right side of the fairway on this 560-yard par 5. It was lying in the so-called "short rough" (always a plus!) and somewhat teed up in the grass. Not only that, I had a clear shot to the green. No trees, water, shrubs—nothing.

To compensate for these ideal conditions, of course, was the pressure they all conspired to heap upon me, as if not letting my brother down and wanting to give a good accounting of myself weren't enough. But I mustered up just enough moxie and dismissed all these pressures just long enough to pull off a beautiful arcing three wood shot that crossed the fairway purposefully and landed maybe fifty yards or so from the green, just short of the rough. From there it was a gentle pitching wedge (see next section) and a careful downhill putt for a birdie. The three wood was the key to the whole thing.

The Pitching Wedge

Sometimes I'll play a game with myself trying to rank order the clubs that give me the most satisfaction when I hit them correctly. Although the three wood and the putter are right up there, the four iron is in the mix, and the sand wedge is, to use a horse racing term, moving up on the outside, no club gives me the kind of satisfaction that I get from hitting a good wedge shot. There is something special about the controlled loft, the option of some backspin, the broad range of distances within which it can be used, and the different effects that can be achieved by changing the angle of the club face.

I must add, though, that I have not mastered this club at all. In fact, during my first summer of playing seriously, I spent a great deal of time at the practice pitching green and thought I'd pretty much become the Wedge Maestro. I was hitting great shots for the rest of the summer after I started practicing. The next summer, assuming that my wedge skills were locked in, I abandoned those practice sessions—and paid dearly. They disappeared like so much dust in the wind, and it has been a struggle ever since. My IPP will even bring it up now and then: "Fitz, you don't hit that wedge like you did in '01," or "I'm still looking for the return of 'The Magic Wedge' from the old days."

Clubs are Trump

This is one club that simply must not be taken for granted. There are so many nuances in a wedge shot that there is only one safe, and very unspectacular, prescription for respecting the potential of this club: practice. If you cannot find a practice green at a nearby course, make one in your back yard or at the city park down the street or in your living room or your recreation room using whiffle balls and a rug scrap. The muscle memory that comes with practicing these shots is fickle enough as it is, given the many possible ways in which to hit a wedge shot; it's like working with at least a half a dozen different clubs all rolled into one. Until you can literally *feel* how the club likes to move, how the club head moves through differing lengths of grass or depths of sand, how your arms like to relate to that movement, how the ball responds at impact, and how it behaves once it lands—you might as well leave the club in your bag. It is a club of immense and uncalculated potential for recreational golfers.

Various instructors and pros offer varying impressive percentages as to how important the so-called *short game* is, but there are two that stand out in my mind: 1) nearly sixty percent of the total number of strokes in an average round are putts and chips, and 2) eighty percent of the total time spent practicing should be spent on short game shots inside one hundred yards. You have to enter into a covenant of no small significance in order to make friends with your wedges. I learned that the hard way, and I now spend a great deal of time and energy trying to repair the broken friendship. I use three wedges: sand, pitching, and lob. They are the most influential trinity in my golf bag.

There are only *two* keys to this type of shot when you want to succeed at trimming strokes:

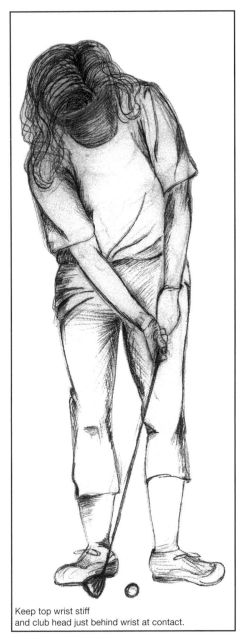

Keep top wrist stiff
and club head just behind wrist at contact.

Key 1
No matter what kind of a wedge shot you're going to attempt, *make sure that you do not let the club head get ahead of your wrists.* This is a common piece of advice for many shots in developing a good short game, but the problem is that your *own* head will not, *cannot*, master this requirement unless and until your arms and hands develop the muscle memory necessary for this type of shot. That may sound obvious, but I cannot begin to describe for you how weird some of the realities of wedge shots feel. You just have to do them until they begin feeling comfortable, until they "come

standard" for you. I remember starting to experiment with wedge shots and watching golf tournaments on television to see what a wedge shot looked like from the point of view of how the golfer's arms moved in relation to the club. I've always learned best by watching and then imitating—I don't respond to the technical language, the drawings, or the drills until I have created a picture of the swing in my head, and that comes from someone doing it in front of me—probably many times. So watch a few tournaments, and pay special attention when golfers are within one hundred yards of the flag stick. Think about these short game shots. Then do them yourself *before* you expect them to happen easily for you on the course. There are all sorts of angles, degrees of swing, bends at the knees or waist, hinging of the wrists, and weight issues involved, and a pro giving you lessons could probably spend a whole summer just on how to use the wedge. The pro at my home course uses a really simple expression for this. He says you have to *"create a feel."* With or without the pro, it's a *"feel thing,"* so keep working with it because it really is an act of creation more than it is an act of development. You will know when it has arrived fully formed, and *then* you can work on its development.

Key 2
Remember to follow through and finish with the club pointing at the target. "Follow through" is an incredibly important skill in life, never mind golf, so when you think about following through on a golf swing, it shouldn't be any big deal.

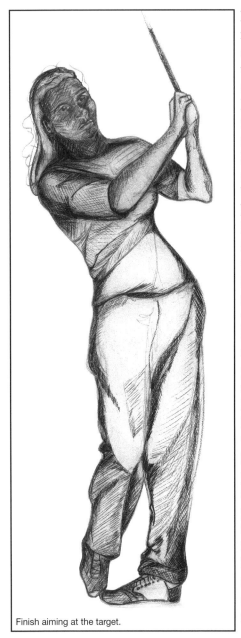

Finish aiming at the target.

Make it second nature, a habit you develop and stick with, a matter of course, automatic. In making wedge shots, concentrate on what it feels like when your shot is finished. Where is your club head pointing? How do your arms feel? Where are you looking? Is the club up high or back behind you somewhere? How has the ball responded? When you practice, you need to make little adjustments in such things as where the ball is in relation to your stance and at what angle you are holding the club face. Try to absorb both how the whole shot feels and, of course, whether or not the ball does what you want it to do. When you start hitting good chips and wedge shots, you won't be able to get enough of them. You'll be like Br'er Rabbit in the briar patch: You'll be saying, "Please, oh, please, *don't* give me another wedge shot!" and meaning just the opposite.

There are two mini-keys I'd also like to mention in connection with using a pitching wedge. One of them is technical, and one of them is mental:

Technical mini-key: keep a stiff left wrist

I cannot remember a single wedge shot that worked for me from in close when I wasn't aware of how stiff I kept my left wrist during the shot. To put it another way, I rarely use the wedge when, as they say in baseball, I can just "swing away." Keeping your left wrist stiff helps to make sure that the first key above occurs, that the club head does not flick past your wrists at any time during the shot. Experiment with this and exaggerate it when you are first trying it out. You should feel a significant amount of control over just how far the ball flies through the air. It's a sort of brake or a governor, if you will, on any free and out-of-control swinging you might be inclined to do.

Mental mini-key: commit to the shot

Make sure you are committing to hitting the shot boldly, squarely, confidently. This will correct for any restraint or holding back that you might subtly be forced into by keeping your left wrist stiff. Chapter 5 deals with the whole subject of commitment, and committing to the shot is on literally every golfer's Top Three list of the most important rules of thumb to keep in mind at all times. You will usually know when you have committed to a shot as quickly as you will know when you have not.

These two "mini" keys go hand in hand. Long ago, I lost count of the stubbed wedge shots I hit because I was not committed to the club I had chosen, to my swing, or to my target. I've heard it said by more than a few people in more than a few ways: Commitment is crucial no matter where your ball ends up on the course or at what distance it is from the flagstick.

The Putter

It should be such an easy club to master. Putting is such a simple motion. It requires so little strength and so little backswing and follow-through. Why, oh why, is it so $@!!^&* difficult? On Sunday, February 11, 2007, I heard Phil Mickelson, who was in the process of winning at Pebble Beach, say he had spent the previous week working on his putting because it had been, as he put it, "atrocious" the weekend before. Mickelson? Atrocious putting? He's a world-class professional. In the spring and summer of 2007, he was ranked sixth in the world for average putts per hole at 1.73. In 2008, his average ballooned to 1.79 putts per hole. How can he be struggling with the same demons that we aspiring bogey golfers are struggling with?

How many times have you heard someone say, "Drive for show, putt for dough"? Do you know what the subtext to this cliché is? Do you know what hidden meaning this little aphorism contains? Here it is in multiple forms and in simple words each time:

* Get to know your putter better than you know any other club.

* Play holes keeping just one thing in mind: no 3-putts.

* Find a putting green to practice on, and make it your home away from home.

* Clear a path on your living room rug, lay a drinking glass on its side, and putt into it from every conceivable distance.

* Play miniature golf. Putt two balls instead of one on the greens when no one is waiting behind you on the course. Or three. Or four.

* Putt each and every putt as if it was for a million bucks.

* Read some *Golf Digest* articles on putting.

* Make up putting games with a partner on the club putting green.

* Show up half an hour before your tee time to practice on the putting green.

* Go to the local golf shop during the off-season, and putt with their demo putters.

* Try putting out of the sand traps just off the greens if there is a "ramp" out of them.

* Putt blindfolded.

* Putt uphill.

* Putt downhill.

* Find the toughest green on the course, go there at dawn or stay through twilight, and putt until you can't put anymore.

* Take a putting lesson.

* Give a putting lesson.

* Watch tournaments on television.

* Watch tournaments at your hometown course. Sit by the greens when you do.

* Cut out little round disks from poster board or shirt cardboards or cereal boxes and lay them on your rug, making a little 3-hole or 4-hole course.

* Invent games..........are you getting the idea?

Develop an intimate relationship with your putter; make it your favorite club.

I can offer only two more or less generic tips for putting besides what I have written above. Again, one is technical and one is mental.

Technical putting tip: keep your head still

After your putter has made contact with the ball, make sure

that you are looking at the *exact* spot where the ball used to be before you look up to see whether it's going in or not (see Chapter 11). If you don't know what I mean or why you should do it, watch a few pros putt on television and don't watch their putters or their golf balls. Watch their eyes and heads. One tip book I read said to just keep looking down until you hear the ball rattle down in the cup.

Mental putting tip: give the putt a chance

Assume you're going to make the putt. In other words, think positive. When he leaves a putt short of the hole, my brother says, "Amateur!!" That's because pros learn to aim just past the hole (unless it's a downhill putt!) and putt just aggressively enough to make sure the ball gets to the hole. It's easier to learn how to soften up a bit than it is to hit it harder. Give the putt a chance.

Finally, just think: putts make up nearly fifty percent of your score. If you have to, you can avoid using every club in your bag except the putter, so no matter how long you've played, no matter how seriously you really want to get to bogey golf, no matter how good a putter you already are, be sure your putter is your best friend every time you play. If you and your putter are not seeing eye-to-eye, if you are not the best of friends, if you have not reached an understanding, if you're at loggerheads, if the two of you need counseling or a trial separation, if you're butting heads or not speaking or going your separate ways or drifting apart or maintaining a respectful distance from one another, you can pretty much forget about bogey golf. It's that simple. As your mind goes, so goes your putting, and as your putting goes, so goes your round.

Chapter Four
Humility

> Confidence, of course is an admirable
> asset to a golfer, but it should be an
> unspoken confidence. It is perilous to
> put it into speech. The gods of golf lie in
> wait to chasten the presumptuous.
> > P.G. Wodehouse

> The more you play it the less you know
> about it.
> > Patty Berg

If you do not yet know that golf will humble you, I'm guessing you haven't played your first round yet. Humbling events are a rite of passage, and they happen early and often. If you're a good enough golfer not only to have passed through the humiliation phase long ago but to have learned how to spare yourself the misery altogether, there may be other books you should be reading by now. Most of us high-handicappers, casual golfers, and tenderfeet are still learning how hard it is, round after round, to carry humility in our golf bags like tees, ball markers, or loose change for the drink cart girl. Humility is a necessary ingredient in the recipe for making bogey golf a habit. The best news is that we don't have to wait very long, or work very hard, before humility and her entourage, The Killer Dees—Disappointment, Doubt, and Despair—show up unannounced on our doorstep for a stay of indeterminate length.

While it may be natural enough to assume pro golfers to be immune to humbling events, to be way too busy with endorsements, tournaments, and retooling their swings to worry about such a mundane thing as humility, keeping half an eye on any given major tournament will usually prove otherwise. Sooner than you might suspect, there will be a classic moment revealing that humility has no glass ceiling. Now, with the advantage of the Internet and sophisticated television coverage, it is relatively easy to see golf's highs *and* lows immediately and for days afterward just by going to the PGA Tour website.

One of the most heart-wrenchingly poignant episodes of a professional golfer having to wear the mantel of humility occurred at the 2006 U.S. Open at the Winged Foot Golf Club in New York. Having already won that year's Masters Tournament at Augusta National and the previous year's PGA Championship, Phil Mickelson was positioned to win his third major tournament in a row when his game mysteriously fell apart on the final hole of the final day. Golf writer T.J. Auclair, Junior Editor for PGA.com, describes Mickelson's collapse:

> With a driver in hand, Mickelson hit a wild push that flew over the trees, caromed off a hospitality tent and came to rest on a patch of trampled-down grass. With trees obstructing his view to the green, Mickelson's overly aggressive nature overcame him and he attempted to hit a miraculous cut around the trees. What ensued was a nightmare.
>
> The ball didn't cut early enough, instead striking a tree and sending the ball back to Mickelson. He managed to pull off the cut the second time around, but overcooked it and wound up with a terrible buried lie in the left greenside bunker. From there, he sent the sand shot through the green and got up and down for double-bogey.

Here is Ken Klavon, writer for the USGA website, describing the scene in the scorer's tent moments after Mickelson finished his round:

> He sat there in the end, away from everyone, the fans, the media, the pressures all removed, insulated by his wife, Amy, and a room filled with two other people. A guard and the scorekeeper, but that didn't matter.
>
> For the better part of nine minutes, Phil Mickelson alternated between a wobble forward, a frequent wipe to the eyes or a heartfelt hug from his wife. He buried his face in both hands, shaking his head repeatedly.

It is difficult to imagine anyone who watched this happen, fan or otherwise, listening to Mickelson speak to the press about it afterward and perceiving him as anything other than a tragic hero, or, to use his own words, "such an idiot." His candid confession is worth reading in all of its unvarnished humility:

> I still am in shock that I did that…I just can't believe that I did that…I am such an idiot. You know, I had…I couldn't hit a fairway all day, I JUST couldn't hit a fairway all day…and I tried to go to my bread-and-butter shot which is just a big baby carve slice on 18 and just get it in the fairway, and I missed it left…and was still okay, wasn't too bad. I just can't believe I couldn't par the last hole…it really stings, you know, as a kid I dreamt of winning this tournament, I came out here and worked so hard, for so many days. Hadn't made a bogey all week…and then bogey the last hole and then even a bogey would

have got me in a playoff. Just can't believe I did
that. This one hurts more than any tournament
because…you know, I had it won. I came out here
a week or two ago in the evenings…just spending
the evenings on the last four holes… thinking
that I would just need to make four pars, you
know there's a good chance that if I could just
make four pars on Sunday, you know, I could do
it…and made a good par on 15, bogeyed 16, and
doubled 18…and so, ah, it hurts because I had it
in my grasp and just let it go…

No excuses, no stiff upper lip, no whining, just sheer
unadulterated humility in the face of a classic unraveling by
a competitor generally acknowledged to be one of the top
five golfers in the world at that time. It's worth noting that
although Mickelson finished below par in both the British
Open Championship and the PGA Championship later
that same summer, his score was a dozen or more strokes
behind winner Tiger Woods in both tournaments. The next
season, 2007, he finished well back in three of the four major
tournaments and even missed the cut in the U.S. Open. In the
matter of humility in this game, no one is really spared, and
this is especially true the more seriously we take our level
of play. It doesn't matter whether we aspire to succeed at
the professional level or just play bogey golf. Moreover, just
because we eventually learn how to become humble, we do
not automatically get let off the hook.

Knowing that a golfer of Mickelson's caliber can be reduced
to abject and enduring humility is more eye-opening than
it is comforting. It's less a matter of our misery loving his
company than it is the recognition that without humility,
without the ability to be at least somewhat self-effacing
when it is required, this game will break us as it has broken

players since the first golf ball was struck. Humility must become familiar enough that it is a good fit when it needs to be, but it cannot be grabbed out of the bag and donned like a nylon shell whenever it starts to rain. Humility is no quick fix. It has to be more like your favorite golf hat, the one you wear rain or shine, the one that has become a part of you whenever you play. When it's cold or rainy, you just pull it down a little tighter; when it's not quite so sunny, you just tilt it back on your head a bit. As with many important attributes of good character, humility serves us best when it resides comfortably and permanently within us and is available to us unconditionally and without fanfare at the appropriate time.

If humility is going to help us chase bogey golf, it has to exist within us at a level requiring only the merest trigger for it to be activated. We cannot suddenly "get humble" in a desperate effort to cut our losses, or turn it on and off like tap water or an electric light. It has to be there when we address the ball, and it has to be there when we make contact. More to the point, it has to be there when an expected or hoped for outcome fails to materialize. Following his U.S. Open free fall, Mickelson made no attempt to rationalize or equivocate in front of the still-befuddled press; he revealed no discomfort at having to speak about the unspeakable.

Like many of the character traits that are not simply helpful but essential in the game of golf, humility will arrive in its own time if it is going to arrive at all. It asks little more than to accompany us out onto the golf course, and it is most content when we rely upon it sparingly. Once we have accepted it as an essential part of our game, we have to be careful not to let it dilute our resolve, our delight in being challenged, or our willingness to take chances every so often. The best place to work on your humility would most likely be at the driving range or on whatever practice putting green you can find.

HUMILITY

Regardless of how much or how little experimentation you do when you practice, mistakes are not just acceptable but encouraged, and you can practice humility the same way you practice the physical skills. After several practice putts, putt one as if great sums of money and prestige rest on the outcome. After several drives from the tee pad, prepare for and execute a drive that must go a required distance out on the range and straight down the middle as if it would guarantee success on *your* final hole at the U.S. Open.

I always like to end a practice round with a successful drive, chip, or putt, but lately I am beginning to think that I should end my sessions with the "last stroke," whether it is a good one or not—just so that occasionally I have to live with the humility that accompanies failure when the last stroke is not as successful as I intended it to be. As the example above illustrates, recovery can often take a very long time when the stakes are very high. See how long it takes for you to "recover" from a bad final shot in the last practice round. While there is no such thing as perfect humility, especially in a sport as challenging as golf, practicing the mental skills that the game requires is no less important than practicing the physical skills.

So much about this game is about balance. You have to balance on your feet after you swing, you have to balance your speed with your line when you putt, and you have to balance your humility with your confidence. The skills required *just* to play bogey golf are prodigious enough that it's time for me again to say that this objective is *not* about learning how to settle for mediocrity. Playing bogey golf is not the equivalent of mediocrity—for us. For pros and scratch golfers, yes, of course. But for us, the "great unwashed," who aspire only to require one extra stroke per hole, this tightrope act between humility and confidence is a challenge of no small dimension.

Here's a little test: play a round without keeping score. Take as many shots as you want, hit as many mulligans as you want, use the foot-wedge as often as you wish. You only have to do one thing: keep track of the number of shots that feel terrific. Drives, irons, fairway woods, chips, putts … just count them and them alone. When your round is done, what was the tally? On a good day, with a little luck thrown in, and giving yourself the benefit of the doubt on the marginally satisfying shots, two or three good shots per hole is doing very well. Were you able to keep that up the whole round? An average of two good shots each hole? Let's say your usual stroke total is in the neighborhood of 50 for nine holes. That means, then, that fewer than half of your shots were satisfying. Half! Try now to imagine doubling whatever that number was. That means that instead of, let's say, eighteen good shots in a score of 50, you're trying to hit thirty-six good shots. Imagine that! That's *par* on most courses.

For most of us, a score like that is unimaginable, but my point is that in a round such as this, we still have fourteen shots remaining to reach our hypothetical score of 50, and we have a generous nine more with which to reach bogey. Aiming just to keep track of the "good" shots gives us a glimpse of how difficult it is even to shoot bogey. So—now—take away the benefit of the doubt, add the pressure of keeping score, no more mulligans or foot-wedges—play by the rules, in short—and try to approach bogey golf with that reminder of how hard it is to succeed on even half of your stroke total.

Humility should be like an invisible fifteenth club in your bag, a "rescue club" more reliable even than your hybrid four iron, your lob wedge, or your chipper. This is the kind of humility that keeps things in perspective for you, not the kind that pummels, judges, or belittles you. It's the kind of humility that allows you to continue to breathe deeply as you walk down the fairway. It's the kind that makes it a matter of course to review the technique you just employed on that last shot and realize that you lifted your head up too soon, or gripped the club too firmly, or did not bring your hip through all the way on the follow through. It's the kind of humility that prevents you from sulking when you're playing poorly, and it keeps you from crowing when you're playing well.

One of the many great stories that Arnold Palmer tells is one about overconfidence—the absence of humility, in other words. Palmer recalls playing the final hole of the 1961 Masters Tournament:

> I had a one-stroke lead, and I had just hit a very satisfying tee shot. I felt I was in pretty good shape. As I approached my ball, I saw an old friend standing at the edge of the gallery. He motioned me over, stuck out his hand and said, "Congratulations." I took his hand and shook it, but as soon as I did, I knew I had lost my focus. On my next two shots, I hit the ball into a sand trap, then put it over the edge of the green. I missed a putt and lost the Masters. You don't forget a mistake like that; you just learn from it and become more determined that you will never do that again. I haven't in thirty years since.

The commercial for the PGA Tour's televised events used to end with the emphatic slogan, "These guys are good!" We have no way of knowing the price each of "these guys" pays for getting that good, but learning how to keep humility and confidence in proper balance must have come into the picture early in their careers or they would not have qualified for the tour. Furthermore, it's probably safe to assume that they each have their own unique relationship to humility, a relationship that does not get in the way and that helps them rally from setbacks no matter how long the rallying takes. Costly lessons, the finest equipment, a season pass and even an IPP—these are only trappings. The hard work of acquiring and practicing humility should be tackled as consistently out of season as in. Learning how to make it a comfortable fit for our playing days is as challenging a job as there is in this chase.

CHAPTER FIVE
COMMITMENT

I expect to pass through this world but
once. Any good, therefore, that I can do
or any kindness I can show to any fellow
creature, let me do it now. Let me not
defer or neglect it for I shall not pass this
way again.

> Stephen Grellet

The harder you work, the luckier you
get.

> Gary Player

The Minnesota Twins began the 2006 summer very badly. By
May 1, they had a record of only nine wins against sixteen
losses. They were nine full games behind the first place Detroit
Tigers, and by June 1, they were 24–29, 11 ½ games behind the
Tigers. On June 13, my IPP and I headed down to Minneapolis
to see them take on the resurgent Boston Red Sox, who
were tied with the Yankees atop the American League East
Division. The Twins were still five games under .500 at 29–34,
a whopping twelve games out of first place in the American
League Central Division

Like many so-called baseball purists, I'm not crazy about the
Twins ballpark in Minneapolis, the Hubert H. Humphrey
Metrodome. It was a novelty in 1982 when domed stadiums
were all the rage, but it is staggeringly remote from the
Friendly Confines, the name Chicagoans and all of baseball
have given the Chicago Cubs' home park, Wrigley Field. The
Metrodome is distinctly unfriendly, with its concrete exterior,

its stiff red poles, even its white crosshatched balloon roof. But on this night, we didn't care about the building. It was all about the game. It was spellbinding, complete with a titanic pitchers' duel pitting Red Sox ace Curt Schilling against Twins ace Johann Santana, a marvelously photogenic, signature bobble by Red Sox left fielder, Manny Ramirez, and a game-winning, grand slam home run by an unheralded substitute young outfielder, Jason Kubel in the bottom of the twelfth inning. The Twins went on to sweep the series with the Sox and begin an epic winning streak.

Why this story about the Twins' winning streak?

My IPP and I often talk about how difficult it must be to play for a team that makes a summer long habit of losing games and plays itself out of contention early in the season. I have heard many athletes talk about what happens when adversity surrounds them: about believing in themselves, being patient, working hard to isolate the problem, and not pressing. Mustering what it takes do all of that day after day can be summarized in one word: *commitment*. If one is committed to a particular task, occupation, skill, or person, quitting is simply not an option, contract notwithstanding. The job surely must become much more difficult, if not unpleasant. But it's no less dependent on a routine or a regimen just because times are tough. It may require additional focus, additional time, even some assistance from outside sources or specialists, but these coping strategies are all embraced as part of the job. They come with the territory, signal a commitment to any and all that are observing, and most important, they signal a commitment to the person him or herself.

That one summer, had the Twins lost hope, it would not have been possible for them to achieve a record of 67–32 after June 13. They would not have earned accolades, headlines, and limitless fan zealotry if they had assumed that they had no shot at the division championship. They certainly would not have clinched their division by edging those very same Detroit Tigers on the last day of the regular season. To the fans, the media, the coaches, and certainly to the Twins players themselves, the fact that the two teams in front of them—Detroit and Chicago—were also winning almost every one of their games during that stretch did not matter.

The second half of the season became its own reward. The resurgence of a team that most fans and sportswriters alike had counted out before even a month of the 2006 season had gone by had become a conversation piece in barber shops and grocery stores, on street corners and talk shows, at shopping malls and places of worship—and golf courses. If you are a Twins fan, you remember what I am talking about here, I am sure. If you are not a Twins fan, you don't necessarily need to become one to appreciate what they accomplished. Checking the record books, there aren't more than a half-dozen such reversals in Major League Baseball's modern era.

The year 2006 gave Twins fans truly a legendary second half of the baseball season, and when it finally came to an end in October—with three straight truly anticlimactic losses to the Oakland As—there was nonetheless a very palpable pride across the state and in the media. We understood the players' own pride and their commitment not just to their profession, but to doing the very best no matter what obstacles were thrown in front of them, no matter how much adversity they had to face, no matter how far behind they fell in a game or in the standings. And just think: all *we* have to do is commit to a simple little golf shot.

When I reflect on such achievements as that one, I often wind up making lists. This is certainly true for this book; you only have to look at the names of the chapters for proof. Every title is an item from a list. One of my favorite topics for a list is this one: What Are the Three Most Important Things to Remember in Golf? There are as many of these lists as there are golfers, I am convinced, but here is mine:

1. Don't get too high or too low during a round.
2. You can't hit a good shot angry or rushed.
3. Whatever shot you're going to hit, commit to it.

Is this list a little too un-technical? Technical advice is like getting too many presents on your birthday, at least the way I look at it. You have to spend a fair amount of time sorting them all out, making sure they all fit or work or have batteries, giving each one the individual attention you know it deserves or requires, and cleaning up the mess after you've unwrapped them all.

I like simplicity, and it is one of the hardest things I have to learn on the golf course. That's why this list is simple, and I offer it as both an alternative and an antidote. It's an alternative to the head, eye, hand, back, and elbow sorts of tips that golfers include in their lists. It's also an antidote for those times when it seems like you are not doing anything correctly on the course, when you feel like your game is coming apart, when you're increasingly certain that *the wheels are coming off the wagon.* (I love that phrase. My IPP and I use it frequently; it seems to capture, in such a graphic way, exactly what happens too often on the golf course.)

The item from the list that I like the best is the third one because it actually incorporates elements of the first two and requires us to think hard about what commitment means—in golf and in life. I remember when my brother and I practiced hitting eight iron bump-and-runs until we'd practically worn paths on the green. I had previously only used a seven iron for that shot. Sometimes I relied on my pitching wedge, but after I discovered the eight iron's versatility with a shot like this, I've doubled the pleasure. I have come to like the shot a great deal in no small part due to having sunk a few from several feet off the green since then. I did, however, go through a long period of time stubbing the iron on that shot almost every time.

Stubbing an iron means that you hit the ground too far behind the ball. This habit is on its very own list of The Most Frustrating Mistakes in Golf. Stubbing shows lack of commitment, pure and simple. It's failing to believe enough in what you're doing to follow through with conviction. It comes from a host of internal breakdowns, and leaves a horrid taste in the mouth, a distinct sense of an egregiously wasted opportunity, and an immediate desire to fling the club—or the whole bag. It's basically inexcusable. It lowers a golfer's self-respect, interest in the rest of the hole, and standing in the group he or she is playing with.

Here's how to avoid stubbing.

Commit to the shot. Period.

Imagine the ball lifting up high enough to travel the distance you want it to and rolling confidently toward the cup, then practice the motion at least three times so that your muscle memory is reactivated sufficiently and you can feel a firm pass through the grass. Here are three small pieces of advice, purely physical, that will maximize your success:

Tip 1: Keep your front arm stiff during the entire shot.

Tip 2: Wherever you stop, make sure you finish pointing at the cup.

Tip 3: Move the club at a steady speed through the ball <u>without</u> decelerating.

Regarding the non-physical part of committing to the shot, believe in the shot once you have decided that it is the best one for this particular lie in these particular conditions and in your particular frame of mind. Make the seven or eight iron or the wedge your very best friend for this shot. Trust it. There may be some risk involved; that's fine. Understand that you may not make it all the way to the cup, or that you may even send the ball past the cup. If you can get it close, you've taken a tremendous amount of pressure off your putter. Understand and believe that you have the skill, the timing, and the judgment to make this deceptively complicated shot without a hitch. If you can do all of these things, you have committed to the shot. I'm not guaranteeing that you won't stub your club if you can do all of this because the shot—the preparation, the conviction, and the commitment—must be yours, not mine.

If you can take this level of commitment to each and every swing, whether you're a beginner or a scratch golfer, you have learned much more than just how to play a solid round of golf. You will have learned that commitment has positive results no matter where you demonstrate it. Driver, three wood, sand wedge, six iron, job, hobby, friendship, those whom you love … and those whom they love, including yourself. It's all part of the same mental and physical partnership that results in good shots in golf and good experiences in life.

CHAPTER SIX
WHEN PLAY IS SUSPENDED:
BUILDING YOUR GOLF LIBRARY

> He furnished me
> From mine own library with volumes that
> I prize above my dukedom.
>
> Shakespeare

> At one point in my life, I was considered to be
> fairly well-read. I often wonder if it was the
> onset of a family, or my dedication to reading
> only books on golf that doesn't allow me to
> make that claim at this point in my life.
>
> Author Unknown

I like to read, so reading an occasional golf book isn't hard to do, and there is an ore boat load of them out there to choose from. While books alone won't get you to bogey, there are a small number of classics that might offer inspiration, motivation, companionship, or comfort during your quest. There are many books—small, medium, and large—that can be helpful if you read them carefully and follow them to the letter. There are far fewer that can address both mental and physical challenges and help you overcome them as you are building your own personal approach to the game. You can build your own library, make your own list, explore your own bookstores, libraries, and pro shops, but I have looked at many (though barely a fraction) of the options and considered which ones will be the most helpful, not just in some day playing bogey golf but enjoying the process as well. So here is my own Top Ten list, followed by annotations and a short annotated Honorable Mention list.

1. The Bible (Old and New Testaments).

2. *The Tao Te Ching* translated by Gia-Fu Feng and Jane English. Vintage Books, 1989.

3. *Flow: The Psychology of Optimal Experience* by Mihaly Csikszentmihalyi. Harper & Row, 1990.

4. *Golf and the Spirit: Lessons for the Journey* by M. Scott Peck. Three Rivers Press, 1999.

5. *Harvey Penick's Little Red Book: Lessons and Teachings from a Lifetime of Golf* by Harvey Penick with Bud Shrake. A Fireside Book, Simon & Schuster, 1992.

6. *The Greatest Game Ever Played: Harry Vardon, Francis Ouimet, and the Birth of Modern Golf* by Mark Frost. Hyperion, 2002.

7. *Golf in the Kingdom* by Michael Murphy. Penguin Arkana, 1972.

8. *Five Lessons: The Fundamentals of Modern Golf* by Ben Hogan. Simon & Schuster, 1957.

9. *Who's Your Caddy?* by Rick Reilly. Broadway Books, 2003.

10. *The USGA Rules of Golf.* The United States Golf Association, 2005.

The Bible

What follows are comments about two chapters of the Bible followed by five other references in list form at the end. After that, you're on your own. I should mention here that I am a lifelong Unitarian with Quaker leanings, which doesn't have anything to do with this chapter except that you need to know that I do not have any axe to grind when it comes to using the Bible as a source, either of inspiration or information. It's just a really good book no matter what your faith is. Reading it, not to mention drawing inspiration from its pages, does not necessarily lead to conversion. Every good story has some lessons to offer receptive readers, and the Bible is no exception.

The Book of Job

Saying that someone has the patience of Job is usually a compliment, and the assumption is that there is no greater patience than Job's. On the golf course, any patience at all is a good thing, and if you can get to the point where you're demonstrating the kind that Job, a God-fearing man who didn't even **play** golf, displayed when God decides to test him, I think it's safe to say that you'll be a worthy match for any scull, shank, or slice you can muster. In the history of golf, there are probably half a dozen or so individuals who have been confronted with setbacks of what we might term "biblical proportion." Most recently, consider Phil Mickelson's collapse in the 2006 U.S. Open (See Chapter 4). All he had to do was make par on the eighteenth hole in Sunday's round, and he didn't do it—thanks, in large part, to making several infamous shots involving a tent, a tree, and a sand trap. There is Greg Norman who has two British Open victories to his credit (1986 and 1993) but who, in thirty years of tournaments, has only eighteen other first place finishes, not one of them a major. He is remembered primarily for his infamous collapse in the 1996 Masters at Augusta National, turning a six-stroke lead on the final day to a five-stroke loss. You can look up the names of Jean Van de Velde (1999 British Open at Carnoustie, Scotland) and Arnold Palmer (1966 U.S. Open in San Francisco) if you need further proof that it happens to the best of us. Van de Velde has since put his very scenic and illustrious meltdown into perspective, but it takes very close to the patience of Job just to watch replays of his triple bogey on the final hole of the only major tournament for which he has ever been in the running.

Read the book of Job, and try to imagine where Job would have finished on the Ten Worst Golf Chokes of All Time list if he'd been a golfer. He would have been in a class by himself. In this famous narrative, God decides to subject the man described as "blameless and upright, one who feared God, and turned away from evil" to relentless suffering and misfortune. He sends the archangel Satan (known universally as a first-class troublemaker) to give Job a really hard time—but not to take his life. It is an experiment, and Job is the guinea pig. The details are many and lengthy, but suffice it to say no expense is spared when it comes to God and Satan seeing what Job is made of. We're not talking inconveniences here, either; we're talking crops failing, children dying, and property destruction. The first two chapters read like a narrative from a biblical boot camp. Along the way, three buddies try to convince Job to repent, to ask forgiveness, to confess, to own up. They challenge his virtue and dignity saying that he *must* have done something to deserve such torment. But, of course, Job has done no such thing, so his pals (Eliphaz, Bildad, and Zophar) come off looking like stooges because they do not (and probably cannot) understand that their friend Job is actually a chosen one.

Finally, "out of the whirlwind," God confronts Job, who has steadfastly, *patiently*, refused to blaspheme, complain, or lose faith all this time. God presents a cataloguing of all of His responsibilities and His omniscience and manages along the way to squeeze in a shorter list of man's shortcomings as well.

Job, who is already quite familiar with the human condition, nevertheless reaffirms his faith, repents of his ignorance of God's power, and generally plays it quite straight in the final confrontation. God restores Job's fortunes, and he lives to be 140 years old and see four generations. Now if that's not patience, I don't know what is.

Being a good golfer requires an inordinate amount of patience. I can't say this any other way. We may not ever become good golfers even *with* patience, but sure as anything, we won't have a snowball's chance in Satan's lair without it. As long as the book of Job is, and enigmatic as some of the lessons are, it's a very good story to keep in mind when your fade turns into a slice or your draw turns into a snap hook. And though it is impossible to outdo the book of Job, you can always look up one of those classic choke jobs from the world of rich and famous golfers and get some reassurance that your troubles pale in comparison.

The Sermon on the Mount

If the book of Job (Old Testament) is a one wood, the Sermon on the Mount (New Testament) is a full bag of fourteen clubs. There is something for everyone in Matthew 5:1–7:29. It begins with what are called the Beatitudes. I will not list them here, but you should be familiar with at least one or two of them. The one I like the best, the one most relevant to the whole concept of playing bogey golf—or at least *aiming* for playing bogey golf—is this one: "Blessed are those who mourn, for they shall be comforted."

"Mourn?" you ask.
Yes, *"Mourn!"*

Don't you mourn after a particularly bad shot? Mourn for the

shot you wasted, mourn for the score that will be at least one
stroke higher because of that shot, mourn for your bruised or
slighted self esteem, mourn for the loss of the perfection you
tried so hard to capture on that shot. "Mourn" it is.

Jesus had a slightly different take in mind, I realize, and one
that addresses much more fully the daily lives of human
beings. Anyone who has lost a loved one, who has been
deprived of something tangible and most dear, who has
failed to achieve a goal will be at least somewhat comforted
by the fourth Beatitude, because comfort is not easy to come
by. Faith in a higher power, no matter what name we give to
it, enables one to mourn rather than despair, to grieve rather
than give up. Through mourning and grief, we can eventually
carry on rather than surrender. Trying to make a connection
between teachings that are 2,000 years old and a puny game
of golf seems the height of either ambition or lunacy. But think
about it again as you listen to the words "Blessed are those
who mourn, for they shall be comforted." It would be easy
to think that the word "comforted" on the golf course means
only "made to feel better." But there is more to these simple
words than superficial comforting. When we allow ourselves
to be comforted, or even to comfort ourselves—which is
always difficult—we also allow ourselves to carry on despite
the loss. When there is no comfort, many things start to
wither: hope, peace of mind, growth, joy, creativity, a sense of
accomplishment, companionship.

There are many other lessons in the Sermon on the Mount,
lessons on anger, serving two masters, judgment (this is
huge!), choosing the easy way out, the Golden Rule, and more.
Not everything is relevant to your golf game, but there is
probably more that is than isn't. Here are five other very short
sections in the Bible you might want to look at and consider; I
leave the annotations to you:

1. Exodus 20:7 (Old Testament)
2. Romans 14 (New Testament)
3. Hebrews 11:1-3 (New Testament)
4. Proverbs 4 (Old Testament)
5. Proverbs 16:1-11 (Old Testament)

Tao Te Ching

The other nine books on this list are fine sources for inspiration or instruction, but this book is the one I'd want if I was marooned on a deserted island—with or without a golf course—and could choose only one. It's also the hardest one to understand. Deceptively simple in language and as relevant today as it was when it was written, it's a daunting challenge to put it into practice in our daily lives, much less in our golf games. You can also throw in the fact that it is the shortest of these books, and it may well be the cheapest if you can find a used copy.

Lao Tsu (or Laozi), a Chinese philosopher, lived six centuries before the birth of Christ. That's 2,600 years ago. Thus, it's safe to say that he didn't play golf—which is probably an advantage—but I'd swear that Lao Tsu knew golf was coming. Most people have heard of Confucius; many fewer are familiar with Lao Tsu. Apparently, the two met for several months (in 6000-something B.C.), and when Confucius returned home, he reported that he had had his mind blown; that is to say, he'd had it illuminated by the older man. Confucius was all about structure and formality and rules in his thinking and his philosophy, whereas Lao Tsu believed in (and lived a life of) utter simplicity in thought and action. One of the many legends surrounding this most influential thinker in Chinese history suggests that we were almost denied ever having the *Tao Te Ching* at all. Lao Tsu, according to the legend, didn't write it down until the very last minute, when someone recognized him as he was leaving his homeland forever. The stranger asked Lao Tsu for a copy of his writings, and Lao Tsu answered that none existed. The man insisted that Lao Tsu immediately write his ideas down, so he dismounted from his buffalo and wrote what we now know as the *Tao Te Ching*.

The edition I use is published by Vintage; the translators are Gia Fu-Feng and Jane English, and the introduction is by Jacob Needleman, professor of philosophy at San Francisco State University. I think this translation is fairly well respected, but others could probably give you the main ideas without too much variation. I spend as much time reading and rereading the introduction as I do Lao Tsu's eighty-one short poems, because I want to understand exactly what Taoism is. It also explains some of the expressions that appear repeatedly, like "the ten thousand things" which is simply an expression for the tangible objects in the universe. The *Tao* also uses the word "source" frequently. Simple as it sounds, it is difficult to grasp because—remember, Taoism is NOT Christianity, nor in any way theistic—we are asked to take it on faith that "the source" (note the absence of a capital S) exists and plays a key role in how the universe unfolds.

Of the many striking sentences in Dr. Needleman's introduction, this one stands out as particularly relevant to the game of golf:

> Our primary and perhaps only true responsibility is to become individuals who are also conduits for the supreme creative power of the universe.

Wow. As we used to say in the '70s, "Can you dig it?"

But some, more befuddled than awestruck, might instead

just ask in wonderment, "What has this got to do with golf?" Though the answer to such a simple and honest question is not at first obvious, it bears some consideration. What Needleman recommends is a hefty responsibility, and it is an especially daunting prospect on the golf course. You don't have to be a pro or even a devotee of the game to know what happens when you take yourself too seriously. Needleman's sentence seems to be addressing that sort of dilemma. If we don't take our game seriously, how will we improve? I don't yet have any firsthand experience with this (not counting inspirational films like *The Legend of Bagger Vance* or *The Greatest Game Ever Played*—see 6 below), but I assume most golfers who play well consistently, professionals or not, know how to keep things in perspective. This sentence is all about perspective. But "conduits"? I thought the word *conduit* referred to electrical piping or an aqueduct or someone who serves as a go-between. All of these may be contained in this quote, so we should consider what this word suggests before looking at a few excerpts from the *Tao*.

If you can manage to apply the concept of less is more to your golf game (see Chapter 2), it will likely emanate from the sort of thinking Lao Tsu encourages in this book. It's certainly possible, perhaps even simple, to understand the thinking behind Lao Tsu's words without reading his book, but however esoteric, lofty, or inaccessible you may think his idea is, take note of the fact that this book is number two on my list.

This is worth a try. We *can* be a conduit for something much greater than we can imagine, and as far as our golf game is concerned, the best part about this is that no one checks on our scorecards. It's not reflected in our handicaps, and we ourselves are the only coaches qualified to help us get there. To be your own conduit requires something extraordinary called Negative Capability (see Chapter 2). The idea is this:

you make your *self* as inconspicuous as possible, as free of an agenda as you can, as dispassionate in thought and action as you are capable of being—in order to become inconsequential amid your surroundings and, thus, to essentially melt into the landscape. Another expression might be to say that it means becoming completely present at each consecutive moment of a given experience.

I should point out here that a little book published in 1982 called *The Tao of Pooh* by Benjamin Hoff gives about as good an introduction to Taoism as I've ever read or heard. You will know how Taoism works if you *just* read the first chapter called, innocently enough, "The *How* of Pooh." Here's a very small sample from a very small chapter in that very small book:

> "Life itself, when understood and utilized for what it
>   is, is sweet ... ."
> "Sweet? You mean like honey?" asked Pooh.
> "Well, maybe not *that* sweet," I said. "That would be
>   overdoing it a bit."

Mentioning this title may seem like cheating on my "here are *ten* books," but not only is this book an ingenious idea, it makes Taoism seem much more secular—which is a good thing when we're trying to apply Taoist thinking to someone's golf game. Find a copy for yourself, read the first chapter, and set it next to your copy of the *Tao Te Ching* in your collection.

Back to the real *Tao*. Here are two poems from Lao Tsu's work. First, Number Sixty-Three:

> Practice non action
> Work without doing.
> Taste the tasteless.

> Magnify the small, increase the few.
> Reward bitterness with care.
>
> See simplicity in the complicated.
> Achieve greatness in little things.
> In the universe the difficult things are done as if they
>   are easy.
> In the universe great acts are made up of small deeds.
> The sage does not attempt anything very big,
> And thus achieves greatness.
>
> Easy promises make for little trust.
> Taking things lightly results in great difficulty.
> Because the sage always confronts difficulties,
> He never experiences them.

Tune in to this poem anywhere, absolutely anywhere, and you will find, not too deeply buried within it, an invaluable lesson about the game of golf. Take just the last two lines. When was the last time you confronted a difficulty in your game? *How* did you confront it? My IPP swings his five iron in his living room all winter long and loves it. He has been having swing problems; he is perfectly willing to acknowledge it, and he even makes fun of it. He swings in the living room in cold weather and out on his front lawn in warm weather. He is confronting his difficulty and does not experience it as a difficulty at all. It is a pleasure for him. (Make sure there is at least a nine-foot ceiling in your practice area before trying this at home, though.)

The first line of the poem suggests that we stop playing in order to improve. That advice is actually more apt than it might seem. How many pros have taken time off when their game has been suffering? In 2004, Tiger Woods spent nine months successfully retooling his swing. Not exactly "non-action," but you get the idea. Last summer, my friend and I played more than one hundred rounds, and there were times when we both felt as though we needed a break. Non action can be an important part of improving your game. It gives you a chance *not* to be frustrated, *not* to be repeating mistakes or bad habits, *not* to be putting the emphasis on the wrong aspect of your game. Practice non action.

Finally, take a look at Number Fifty Six:

> Those who know do not talk.
> Those who talk do not know.
>
> Keep your mouth closed.
> Guard your senses.
> Temper your sharpness.
> Simplify your problems.
> Mask your brightness.
> Be at one with the dust of the earth.
> This is primal union.
>
> He who has achieved this state
> Is unconcerned with friends or enemies,
> With good and harm, with honor and disgrace.
> This therefore is the highest state of man.

Compare this poem to Keats's 1817 Negative Capability letter in Chapter 2. You should find some startling similarities between these two very different works. It's probably safe to say (and Lao Tsu would say this as well) that reaching this state, however simply it may be expressed, is something that can rarely be completed in a lifetime, let alone before golf season begins. It's probably also safe to say, however, that there is no better time to begin that process than today.

Flow: The Psychology of Optimal Experience—Steps Toward Enhancing the Quality of Life by Mihaly Csikszentmihalyi

There is hardly a golfer among us—or sports fan—who does not identify to some degree with the concept of flow. Mihaly Csikszentmihalyi, of the University of Chicago, has practically cornered the market of research on flow. I remember first reading an article he published on flow in the mid-'70s, when I was just entering my second decade of teaching. Coupled with George Leonard's *The Ultimate Athlete,* I immediately thought that I understood physical education and sports completely and could not possibly experience unpleasant outcomes ever again.

That was *before* I took up golf.

Now, going back into Csikszentmihalyi's book for some grounding in the psychology of the so-called flow experience, or as he puts it, the optimal experience, I see countless applications to the game of golf. One must first understand that an optimal experience is something entirely different from just going with the flow. Briefly, experiencing flow in an optimal experience comes when one is completely detached from any possible outcome (score, win or loss, statistic) and can experience the activity purely and simply as play. Countless numbers of athletes from diverse sports and games have recounted how they have been in a zone or experienced a heightened form of bliss or performed at peak in some particular competition. In more than thirty years of research, Csikszentmihalyi documents moments like these from the lives of people in every conceivable pursuit. Here is a short excerpt from a chapter called "Cheating Chaos" in which the author considers the accomplishments of the renowned rock climber, Yvon Chouinard:

> Achieving this unity with one's surroundings is not only an important component of enjoyable flow experiences but is also a central mechanism by which adversity is conquered. In the first place, when attention is focused away from the self, frustrations of one's desires have less of a chance to disrupt consciousness … by paying attention to what is happening around oneself instead, the destructive effects of stress are lessened.

If you can survive the heady, challenging language of academic research, this book will go a long way toward helping you establish a kind of psychic detachment which seems to help most competitors when they strive simultaneously for success and focus in completing some athletic and physically demanding task. These competitors either state directly or suggest indirectly that positive outcomes occur in direct proportion to one's ability to achieve "enjoyable flow experiences."

Golf and the Spirit: Lessons for the Journey by M. Scott Peck

This is the first book I read about golf. I did not actually read it; I listened to it as a book on tape. I found myself almost mesmerized by reader Michael Kramer's voice and by picturing the holes, the swings, the moods, and the landscapes that Peck, a sort of coach-caddie-comrade-counselor, escorts the reader through on a fictional eighteen-hole course. Kramer captures a workable blend of detachment and reverie in his interpretation, which was helpful when I began to read the book itself. This is Peck's thirteenth book, and he takes on some of the more heady and ambiguous topics of modern life in the book's nineteen chapters.

You don't have to be a golfer to be intrigued by "Human Nature" (Hole 5), "Paradox" (Hole 8), "Golf and Sexuality" (Hole 15), or "God" (Hole 18). Admittedly, all this psychological material complicates an already complicated and mystifying sport. Slowly, though, with sentences like this one, Peck puts us at ease:

> While you will miss out on much of golf if you regard it as a purely linear sport, you will also miss badly if you fail to pay attention to its lines…you must *aim* each and every shot.

In the chapter entitled "Competition" (Hole 13), Peck takes great pains to explain the business of handicapping and emphasizes the fact that handicapping is one of golf's truly unique features: a way to level the playing field for those of us who are not professional. One's handicap begins to sound like a rite of passage, a privilege, an obligation, an identification card. Furthermore, it is not static. We are not only supposed to tend it, we are supposed to sacrifice for it. Here is Peck on the ritual of earning a handicap:

> No one is simply entitled to a handicap in golf. You must work to get one and work to keep it.

Scarcely a page later, he draws a fanciful parallel between handicapping and affirmative action.

> I seriously think that if those on opposite sides of the [affirmative action] debate were to take a good look at the phenomenon of handicapping in golf, the light would increase and the heat diminish.

A much more civil system of affirmative action would be to handle disadvantage and privilege, or high and low performance the way they are handled in golf. The object is, over time, to lower the handicap with consistent effort and thus become more competitive in the rarified milieu of low handicap golfers. Golfers who care enough about their game to work on it benefit from the company of better golfers, and the handicap system facilitates that.

Peck's seventeenth hole is called "In the Flow." This is my favorite because he relies for much of the chapter on the *Tao Te Ching*. He could easily have brought in Csikszentmihalyi, too. The chapter ranges across Eastern and Western religion, covers what flow experiences can be, and gives a few examples from his own golfing career of more than thirty years. As often as my IPP and I have used the expression, "Go for it," Peck captured all of my attention with this comment about going for a perfect shot:

> There have been four—and only four— occasions in my career as a mediocre golfer when my instinct did not coincide with my limitations. Instead an inner "voice" within me said, "Go for it," and I felt absolutely certain that I could—that I would make that perfect shot.

Golf and the Spirit is accessible in both the pick-out-a-chapter approach and the cover-to-cover approach. What a victory it would be, score notwithstanding, to remain as focused over the course of eighteen holes of golf as Peck is in this remarkable and very versatile eighteen holes' worth of prose.

Harvey Penick's Little Red Book: Lessons and Teachings from a Lifetime in Golf by Harvey Penick

Very few of us duffers knew who Harvey Penick was before the 1995 Masters Tournament. That all changed when Ben

Crenshaw bent over with his head in his hands after defeating Davis Love III by one stroke to win his second Masters. Penick, Crenshaw's friend and coach, had died just seven days earlier. Three years before that, Penick had published this book with the help of fellow Texan Bud Shrake. As he explains in the first chapter, "My Little Red Book," it's simply a gussied-up version of the notebook he began carrying with him in the 1930s. Before considering publication, Penick explains, he had shown it to just one person—his son, Tinsley.

There are some who say *this* book is the only one you need if you're serious about your golf game. It's almost the golfer's version of the *Tao Te Ching*, believe it or not. Here are three short quotes to demonstrate what I mean:

1. The important question is not how good your good shots are—it's how bad are your bad ones?

2. In competition you must be yourself.

3. Playing golf you learn a form of meditation … Golf has probably kept more people sane than psychiatrists have.

Throughout the book, Penick refers to golfers whom he coached—Ben Crenshaw and Tom Kite—and golfers whom he both watched and played with such as the legendary quartet of Ben Hogan, Byron Nelson, Sam Snead, and Jack Nicklaus. Penick assumes we know what he's talking about on every page, so it's pretty much a no-nonsense crash course. We are fortunate beyond measure to have this little gem of a book as a source of inspiration and instruction, not to mention as a lasting memorial to this most genuinely humble professional.

The Greatest Game Ever Played: Harry Vardon, Francis Ouimet, and the Birth of Modern Golf by Mark Frost

This book is truly fine history. It's the story of amateur Francis Ouimet, who overcame tremendous obstacles to gain entry into the field at the 1913 U.S. Open in Brookline, Massachusetts, and then won a five-stroke victory over British professional Harry Vardon. (In the 2005 film of the same name, director Bill Paxton's own son plays the role of the young Harry Vardon). Caring about golf history is admittedly not a high priority for most bogey golfers, but who among us is not touched in some way or another by underdog stories? This one is not only true, it is one of the few such golf stories that is more compelling than the most imaginative of fictional stories; it is also extremely well researched and written. Mark Frost is a multi-talented writer; his screenplay credits also include television shows from three consecutive decades such as *The Six-Million Dollar Man, Hill Street Blues,* and *Twin Peaks.*

Rather than recount all of the facts of this most amazing and unlikely match up from a bygone era, here are two short excerpts that will hopefully reveal the drama of the match and the quality of Mark Frost's writing.

1911 British Open

> Harry turned back the clock that afternoon; his swing flowed like music again. Every shot planned and carried out with precision, no jitters on the green, putts dropped as gently as eggs in a basket, a perfect textbook round. As he advanced, the crowd felt swept up in the wave of an inevitable outcome; the victory they'd been afraid to hope for appeared to be at hand. Massy tried gamely to mount a rally, but Harry gave

him nothing close to an opening. By the fifteenth hole, his lead had grown to eleven strokes. On the seventeenth green, the Frenchman threw in the towel—unheard of in stroke play, particularly in a championship. As Harry prepared to putt, Massy walked over and offered his hand in surrender, then in a grand, Gallic gesture held Harry's hand aloft. The crowd went mad.

1913 U.S. Open

He stroked the first putt to within nine inches of the hole. As he followed it down, the shouts and cries and whoops increased tenfold again. They finally broke through his impregnable concentration, the veil that had covered and protected Francis from the first green onward shattered and fell away from him. As he stood over that nine-inch putt, his entire body began to tremble like a leaf. Shivering so hard, he could barely hold the putter still in his hands.

I am about to become the national champion.

Francis stepped back for a moment, looked up at the sky, looked over at Eddie, looked at the mob scene around him, and could not remotely comprehend where he found himself.

"One more stroke, Francis," said Eddie, at his side. "Just one more."

Though nearly a century has elapsed since these two gentlemen golfers met, it is difficult not to equate some of the most heroic victories of our own time with this classic story, to think of it as a true story for the ages. This record is not only the account of two exquisite golfers in a classic match-up; it is also about their heroic individual efforts on both sides of the Atlantic Ocean to prevail against circumstances far more challenging than a simple golf tournament. For that reason alone, it is well worth the reading.

Golf in the Kingdom by Michael Murphy

I am still puzzled as to whether or not Mr. Shivas Irons of Burningbush Links in Scotland is or was a real person.

Though it takes a while to realize this book is fiction, you never, for a moment, lose touch with its authenticity. It's so believable … Shivas Irons. The name has a mythic quality about it … shrouded in mist, ancient, and mythical. Before twenty pages have gone by, Mr. Irons is working his way into your psyche, making you more than a little self-conscious about your golf game, making you wish you could play a round with him not for the clarity of the instruction but for the showmanship. Author Murphy amplifies the intangible qualities of Mr. Irons and his game so that it reads very much like mythology, yet the emphasis on accessible instruction in the technical and mental aspects of the game leaves you quite breathless with anticipation for the next chapter and for your next opportunity to put some of these keys to work.

A good friend gave me this book with the simple statement that this would be the best golf book I would ever read. You've no doubt noticed that I have said as much about three or four on this list already, but in this case I am quoting a fellow golfer and friend as passionate about his game as he is about his reading. The following glimpse into the mystical quality of Shivas Irons and his manner is but a taste; it should be enough, however, to lure you into its Scottish spell:

> A smile began to form on his face, spreading slowly as if the muscles around his mouth had grown stiff. His eyes looked straight into mine, they were not crossed at all. "Do ye na' ken ye're flyin' heer like a kite—wi' nae mair than a thread holdin' ye?" He raised his muscular hands and snapped an imaginary string between them. "We're all kites in the wind," he said. And off he went into a trance again.

I will soon read this book for a third time. It has just the kind of tension between the ethereal and the grounded that I like in a story, and when it's a book about a sport that demands both qualities, reading it is certain to be a win-win proposition.

Five Lessons: The Modern Fundamentals of Golf by Ben Hogan

When I was growing up in the early 50s and eating my Wheaties, I kept seeing Ben Hogan's name on trading cards on the back of Wheaties boxes and in the local newspapers I was just beginning to take an interest in reading. I wish I had started playing golf back then; had I done so, I would likely now be touting some aspect of the game that is held in somewhat higher esteem than bogey.

I shouldn't have waited for parental encouragement, the inspiration of a close friend, or the opportunity to caddy at the local country club. The only thing required would have been to read five issues of my 1957 *Sports Illustrated* subscription dating from March 11 through April 8. These are Hogan's Five Lessons. They were later compiled into this book, and they are extraordinary because Hogan confesses to not having the

Patty Berg, Ben Hogan, and Sam Snead were three of the athletes whose images inspired youngsters in 1952. Reprinted with the permission of General Mills.

ideal temperament for a teacher. He makes a point of saying that he needs to spend all of his waking hours preparing for and thinking about upcoming tournaments. Therefore, we are fortunate that Sidney L. James (then the *Sports Illustrated* Managing Editor whose foreword is inspiring in its own right) persuaded Hogan to team up with golf writer Herbert Warren Wind and artist Anthony Ravielli to produce this series of lessons.

As technical as these lessons are, they are both interesting and uniquely uncomplicated. The drawings somehow seem so much more accessible than photographs, and I can still to this day recall seeing them appear in my spring issues of *SI* back in 1957. At that point, golf seemed like a foreign language to me. Now, I relish this little manual as much as any I possess. Listen to the stern yet entirely mindful and reassuring tone of Hogan's language on a very common problem and its solution:

> Say a golfer picks his head up and mis-hits his shot badly. His partner will usually tell him, "You didn't keep your head down," as if this were the true cause of the poor shot. It isn't. The true cause was some faulty movement in the golfer's swing that made him pull his head up. For example, if the golfer starts down from the top with his shoulders or his hands and not with his hips, he can't possibly hold his head where it should be. If you are swinging correctly, on the other hand, you can't look at anything but the ball.

A sort of grandfatherly tone emerges from these lessons. Ben Hogan was an original; this book reveals that as much as any historical record might. No matter how old (or young) you are or what your handicap is, take some time to relish and learn from this marvelous collaboration. Selecting it for this chapter over other glitzier, more recent books by sexier golf heroes was not difficult at all.

Who's Your Caddy? : Looping for the Great, Near Great, and Reprobates of Golf by Rick Reilly

Though it may be hard to find sometimes, golf does have an inherently funny side, and there are quite a few funny books available. I'm choosing Rick Reilly to hold down the humor spot in my Top Ten list because he is irreverent, insightful, witty, exceedingly well-informed, and completely unfazed by famous and not-so-famous athletes. Reilly is a former columnist for *Sports Illustrated* and a frequent contributor to ESPN Radio.

I first became a Rick Reilly fan after reading his collection of columns entitled *The Life of Reilly* published in 2000. It wasn't long before I heard him interviewed fairly frequently on sports talk shows hosted by Jim Rome and Dan Patrick. He gives a great interview, and, apparently, the man can play; according to his website, he has a 7 handicap.

Reilly also knows how to schmooze. Among the golfers he caddies for in this book, John Daly, David Duval, and Jack Nicklaus stand out, but he doesn't stop at golfers. He plays rounds with Bob Newhart, Donald Trump, and Deepak Chopra. No golf autobiography would be complete without referencing Augusta National, and Reilly includes a chapter about the 2001 Masters (the one Tiger Woods won for his fourth consecutive major). Reilly caddies for Tommy Aaron, a sixty-four-year-old former Masters winner, and every hole is an adventure. Early in the tournament, Reilly has trouble understanding why Aaron expects him to bring the golf bag to him instead of just a club, so he eventually asks Fred Couples's caddy, Joe LaCava. And Joe LaCava says simply, "Because he is a professional golfer."

Reilly tells us, "I didn't know what that answer meant then. But I'd learn. I'd learn."

At the thirteenth hole, Reilly is introduced to a historic, out of the way shrub at the back of the tee box known among the Augusta National elite as "the pee bush." Visiting the bush "set back in the azaleas and the dogwoods," he imagines decades of history at the spot:

> …it hit me that some of the great names in golf history—Jones, Snead, Hogan, Nicklaus—had all squirted on this very bush. It made me proud. It also made me want to throw out my shoes the first chance I got.

Reilly makes a point of telling us that, despite his best efforts, he was never able to caddy for Tiger Woods. In spite of the trademark scowl and legendary focus, however, I'm betting that it will happen sooner or later because Woods does have a sense of humor. Reportedly, upon being asked why Reilly would not be given the opportunity to make a fool of himself in front of Woods as his caddy for the day, Woods' answer was terse—and funny: "Because … I suck. I need good help."

With Reilly, you feel like you are sitting with a small group of very good friends in a noisy but secluded bar on a remote beachfront resort, or maybe in a skybox at (insert name of favorite ballpark). He's telling you story after story with scarcely a moment either for a sip or a breath, and you wish you had a tape recorder because you know you're going to want to retell these stories to your friends, and because although you're absolutely certain that he's embellishing the truth a little bit, it doesn't matter. The truth resides in these funny, *really funny,* stories just enough to make this collection quite memorable.

The Rules of Golf
by the United States Golf Association (USGA)

I remember it very well: July 19, 2006. Fourteenth hole at Lester Park Golf Course in Duluth, Minnesota. Wednesday morning in the middle of the hottest July on record in Duluth. Three of us. Both my partners are on the green, one nearly twenty feet from the hole and the other less than four feet from the hole. My ball is off the green, *but* it is only about six or seven feet from the hole. The close partner marks his ball and picks it up, and I say to the other partner on the green, "Go ahead." The first fellow says, "It's your play!" Confused, I quickly scroll through the many conversations I have had on this rule. I reassure myself, without looking it up in the rule book, that we all agree that the player whose ball is farthest away from the cup plays first *whether or not the ball is on the green.*

So I say, "I think we agreed…" and before I finish, my more experienced friend says, "You think, but I *know*. You're up."

I stand still, but I feel a slow burn rising inside because I am almost positive that in golf, the ball described in the rule book as being "away" is *farthest* away *whether or not* that ball is on the green. I go ahead and play, but I clearly remember saying to myself, *"This is not over!"* and before I know it, the rest of the round goes into the tank. Later, I found the rule on the Internet, and I emailed the offending partner with my icy, understated disdain for his treating me so rudely in front of another friend. The rule, 10.2b, is very simple…and I was right. Recreational golfers (like me and my two pals, for instance) need to remember that when they're scattered all around, on or off the green, the ball "farthest from the hole is played first." Period.

If Mr. Farthest from the Cup had wanted to defer to me since I was still off the green and, by rule, the flag must stay in the cup until all balls are on the green, he may choose to do that in a friendly game.

Shortly after this incident, I located a copy of the rules to carry in my bag. Almost everyone I play with knows the rules better than I do, but I know *this* one now. Knowing rules is kind of like knowing your wild mushrooms; if you want to pick them, know *one* perfectly, so you'll never make a mistake with it. Then, learn another one, and another. In short, *The Rules of Golf* are not only for tournament players, and knowing most if not all of these rules cannot help but improve your confidence and your game.

Five Honorable Mentions

1. *The Ultimate Athlete* by George Leonard

2. *Be the Ball: A Golf Instruction Book for the Mind* by Charlie Jones and Kim Doren

3. *Caddy For Life: the Bruce Edwards Story* by John Feinstein

4. *How I Play Golf* by Tiger Woods

5. *The Inner Game of Golf* by W. Timothy Gallwey

There are probably as many honorable mentions as there are golfers. This, then, is my not so subtle way of encouraging you to make up your own list if and when you find a few of your own honorable mentions.

Though it is not on this list, I am particularly fond of a letter written by English poet John Keats to his brothers George and Thomas, dated Sunday, 21 December, 1817. The key portion of this document is in Chapter 2. It is so far removed from the world of golf that it demonstrates perfectly how relevant the game of golf can be to a person's life off the course if he or she chooses to let it be so. Keats might have seen the oxymoron in "negative capability" in the writings of Lao Tsu, but in such a short life (he died at the age of twenty five), he must have conceived it himself. Golf was still very much in its infancy during Keats's lifetime, but though there is no record of the poet ever attempting to play the game, had he been given the opportunity, he may well have made a fine bogey golfer.

Speaking of great golfers, I suppose it could be argued that mastering Tiger Woods' instruction book might enable one to play like the man, but there are tour professionals of nearly legendary status who can't come anywhere close to doing that, so I guess we can assume that neither Tiger's secrets nor his lifelong passion nor his peculiar gifts are captured in this book. After all, there is golf, on the one hand—and then there is the unique version that Tiger Woods plays; the twain may never meet.

I read George Leonard's book when it first came out in 1975 and resolved right then to take a new approach to athletics and competition. I'm still trying. It's an easy read and contains theories and examples from a wide variety of athletic endeavors, which should underscore the fact that some of the mental aspects of golf can in fact be experienced in almost any other sport or game. One of Leonard's primary areas of focus is aikido, a martial art form built around joining one's own exertion in combat with that of the opponent, thereby protecting him from harm. At the leading edge of '70s alternative thinking, Leonard teamed up with Stewart Brand, founder of *The Whole Earth Catalog*, to develop New Games, an inclusive kind of competitive gamesmanship where cooperation takes precedence over competition. The slogan of the New Games Foundation is still "Play Hard, Play Fair, Nobody Hurt."

Timothy Gallwey broke onto the sports psychology scene with his 1974 book, *The Inner Game of Tennis.* I remember it being all the rage when it was first published, and I also remember assuming that anything "inner" was out of my league. Tennis is forehand and backhand, isn't it? Just like golf is driving, chipping, and putting. Gallwey's golf book came out for the first time in 1979, so if longevity counts for anything, and if an "inner" game would help your "outer" game, this is probably as good a resource as any there is.

If you want heartwarming and insightful nonfiction, John Feinstein's book about Tom Watson's late caddy, Bruce Edwards, is probably a good choice, maybe the best choice. If you know anything at all about golf history, you know that Edwards was diagnosed with Lou Gehrig's Disease (ALS) in 2003 and died in 2004. He continued to caddy until the strain was too much for him.

I added *Be the Ball: A Golf Instruction Book for the Mind* as much for the title as for its brief snippets of wisdom from a wide variety of golfers—and a few entertainers. I sometimes imagine that it would be fun to be the ball and know the joy of arcing a path over a gentle landscape under a bright blue sky, then finishing with a long comfortable roll. I'd like to feel the subtle contours of a green under my belly and know the finality of dropping into the hole. The best quote I found in this book is from Jean Van de Velde, runner-up at the 1999 British Open. He offers this tidy little bit of insight: "Losing the British Open was not the end of the world. It is, after all, still just golf."

Sure it is, Jean.

Chapter Seven
The Head Thing

My head is on straight,
Most of the time …
                    Bob Dylan

For this game you need, above all things, to be
in a tranquil frame of mind.
                    Harry Vardon

With apologies for the dated and old-fashioned gender
specificity in the following, I submit for your consideration at
the beginning of this chapter about our heads and the game of
golf, this famous 1895 poem by British poet, Rudyard Kipling.
Though most noted for books like *The Jungle Book, Kim* and
Just So Stories, Kipling was a favorite among 1950s dads and
high school English teachers for this highly stylized and
deliberately motivational masterpiece of turn-of-the-century
thinking:

If
If you can keep your head when all about you
Are losing theirs and blaming it on you;
If you can trust yourself when all men
            doubt you,
But make allowance for their doubting too;
If you can wait and not be tired by waiting,
Or, being lied about, don't deal in lies,
Or, being hated, don't give way to hating,
And yet don't look too good, nor talk too wise;

If you can dream—and not make dreams
　　　your master;
If you can think—and not make thoughts
　　　your aim;
If you can meet with triumph and disaster
And treat those two imposters just the same;
If you can bear to hear the truth you've spoken
Twisted by knaves to make a trap for fools,
Or watch the things you gave your life
　　　to broken,
And stoop and build 'em up with worn
　　　out tools;

If you can make one heap of all your winnings
And risk it on one turn of pitch-and-toss,
And lose, and start again at your beginnings
And never breath a word about your loss;
If you can force your heart and nerve and sinew
To serve your turn long after they are gone,
And so hold on when there is nothing in you
Except the Will which says to them: "Hold on";

If you can talk with crowds and keep
　　　your virtue,
Or walk with kings—nor lose the
　　　common touch;
If neither foes nor loving friends can hurt you;
If all men count with you, but none too much;
If you can fill the unforgiving minute
With sixty seconds' worth of distance run -
Yours is the Earth and everything that's in it,
And—which is more—you'll be a Man, my son!

I don't know about you, but in my life the references to a
person's head have been many and varied. From high school

The Head Thing

sports and an "old school" dad to classrooms full of middle school, high school, and college students during my teaching career, I would have to say that the old noggin has been far and away the most referenced of all body parts… and usually in humorous, often somewhat sarcastic, even highly critical ways. Do any of these old standbys ring a bell for you?

> "You'd forget your head if it wasn't screwed on tight!"
> "You ought to have your head examined!"
> "Heads up!"
> "Get your head in the game!"
> "Where was your head on that play?"
> "Keep your head on your shoulders!"
> "Start using your head for something besides a hat rack!"
> "What was going through your head?"
> "Keep your head up!"
> "Don't let it go to your head!"
> "You'd be fine if you didn't have such a swelled head!"
> "Get your head out of the sand!"
> "He's a head case."

Kipling's self-styled mantra about keeping your head "while all about you are losing theirs" is a great way to begin thinking about how important your head is in this game, especially if you have aspirations of playing, er, a bit above your head. I can't begin to count the number of different places in my life where I have had to remind myself to keep my head down. I did not serve in the armed forces, so I never had to crawl under barbed wire while bullets were whizzing overhead, where I'd have to keep my head way down to keep from getting sliced or hit. But I *have* hit my head on more things in my life than I can list for you here. I think the number of hits I've taken topside has actually begun to cloud my memory about how many there actually have been, where or when they took place, how long it took me to recover, or what I yelled at impact. The car door, the basement beams, the furnace pipes, the plant shelf in the kitchen, the low branches out in the yard as I was cutting the grass, the corner of the kitchen cupboard … I've had more than the requisite number of chances to learn to keep my head down, and I freely admit that it is *still* a work in progress.

No single bit of schooling on the practice tees or in the living room or at a lesson is as important as this one: **Keep your head down**. It should be relatively easy to do—especially if you've had a few run-ins with a furnace pipe or an oak branch. Somehow, though, any time you see someone on the golf course zinging a shot way off center, or topping the ball so badly that it doesn't make it past the end of the tee box, chances are better than even that it was head movement that caused the problem.

After my first summer of more or less regular rounds of golf, I came up with an idea—probably not original, though I had not heard it before—for keeping my head still. Every time I settled into my stance, and before I started my swing, I tried to imagine a taut wire running from my forehead through the top of the ball and anchored to the tee. A simple little mind game, yes, but most of the time it works when I remember to do it. The next step, of course, is to keep the wire taut during your swing. In order to get the hang of it, a few other things may have to take a back seat until keeping the wire taut becomes second nature, until you do it without thinking about it. But if you can set or lock in this habit early on, you've established a foundation that will help you through all sorts of other trials and tribulations.

If you watch enough golf matches on television or at local

tournaments, and if you pay attention to the way golfers hold their heads during their swings, you should see this very fundamental element of good golf in action (or, more accurately, inaction). It is especially evident when the television network camera people show us slow-motion footage of a particular player's swing. If you concentrate *just* on the player's head when the camera shows the swing, you will see it looking down at the ball before, during, and just after the club strikes the ball. It sort of looks funny at first, but then you realize that it is so absolutely critical to a good golf shot that it begins to take on a beauty all its own. Think of it: the whole torso has a rotation-thing going, the legs have a bend-and-shift-the-weight-thing going, the arms have a swooping windmill windup-and-travel-360 degrees sort of thing, the club is definitely on the move, and there, in the midst of it all, is the head calmly staying in one place, a kind of eye-of-the-storm control tower.

Look at it this way: a teaching pro or a video or a bunch of how-to-do-it manuals can say all they want about the technical aspects of the game. But how many different ways can someone tell you to keep your head down? That's pretty much the only way to say it: *Keep your head down!* But hold on! There's another part of this that has to go without saying before you're really in the game, a part that should be obvious, but I'd better mention it just in case you're taking what I say too literally. When you keep your head down, it should follow ("as the night [follows] the day," in Shakespeare's words) that you will also *keep your head still*.

Play a few holes just concentrating on whether or not your head moves during your swing. See how long you can keep looking down after you hit the ball. Make your head wait until it has no choice but to turn upward, when your arms and upper body are winding up at the end of your follow-through.

I will guarantee you this: there is a palpable thrill and a sense of deep down satisfaction when you hit your first really solid shot during which you have concentrated solely on keeping your head down and still. If you have been playing for many years, and you know what this is all about, congratulations. Share the wealth. I would have to say that aside from not gripping the club too tightly, and keeping your eye on the ball, this is the lesson that will mean the most to young or beginning or struggling golfers. I remember it as one of my two most memorable so-called "A-ha! moments."

There's a deeper connection that needs to be considered here: think about stillness. Keeping your mind still during a particular golf swing is as critical to success as keeping your head still.

When my IPP and I are having trouble with our swings, we will often say to each other rather bluntly:

> "You were probably thinking too much."

Rarely, if ever, do we disagree on this. If you play any sport at all, especially if it's an individual sport, you are no doubt familiar (perhaps uncomfortably so) with the consequences of thinking too much or thinking at the wrong time, trying too hard, pressing, being tight or locked up, whatever. I am sure that even though I cannot quote chapter and verse, whole squadrons of golf pros and golf writers have put it something like this:

> Think about the shot *before* you hit it, but don't think about the shot *while* you're hitting it.

In the *Tao Te Ching* (see Chapter 6), the first two lines of meditative poem sixty three are these:

The Head Thing

Practice non action.
Work without doing.

You're scratching your head, at this point, wondering how to practice non action in the tee box when all your experience tells you that a golf swing is nothing *but* action. As the poem advises a few lines farther down:

See simplicity in the complicated.

In order for me to see simplicity within any given golf shot, a *very* complicated thing for sure, it is utterly (though often frustratingly) critical for me to be still within my head. This isn't *just* about there being no head motion in my swing, it's about clearing my head of *all* distractions. This pretty much means *all* thoughts, memories, questions, fantasies, lingering doubts, theories about the meaning of life, and, and, and … for the duration of the swing.

There is a very apt phrase that actor Kevin Costner repeats several times in the 1999 film, *For the Love of the Game*. Costner plays Billy Chapel, an aging baseball pitcher who is attempting to resurrect his major league career. In order to dismiss or tune out or ignore the distractions that surround a pitcher in a baseball game, he repeats this mantra to himself:

Clear the mechanism.

But what's "the mechanism"? For a pitcher, it is nothing less than the total physicality of winding up and delivering the pitch right to the center of the catcher's mitt in such a way that the batter has no chance to hit the ball. For a golfer, it is merely (again) the physicality of addressing the ball, taking the club back and moving the club through the plane, striking the ball, and following through. There is no cognition involved in these actions—or there *should* be no cognition involved in these actions—because all the thought has been done beforehand. The phrase "clear the mechanism" means to let the physical act happen uninterrupted. It means to perform an action *without* cluttering it up with any thinking, and thereby to avoid skewing, sabotaging, or compromising that action.

> Practice non action.
> See simplicity in the complicated.

This may all sound like so much Zen jargon, but anyone who plays golf in the least bit regularly, not to mention successfully, can tell you in his or her own words exactly what this is all about. And you only have to play a few rounds in which you are all wrought up in the thought process, hole after hole, or even shot after shot, spraying shots all over the golf course, before you understand that, critical as the mind is in this game, you have to be able to turn it off when the situation demands it. Usually, that situation is when your body is about to take charge. The body and the equipment need to team up to get a job done, and they cannot do it if the head gets in the way.

There's another aspect of the head thing to consider. Just as it is important not to let physical distractions and too much thinking into your head when making a shot, it is also important not to let two other things into your head as well: 1) negative thoughts, and 2) other people's words. My IPP and I talk about getting into each other's heads when we play. Another friend refers to it as "getting in the other guy's kitchen." I like that. Where the cooking gets done. Central control! When my friend and I start yakking back and forth, it's mostly kidding around. After five seasons together, we know when it's happening, and we know it's mostly all in fun. We also know that when we are playing badly, we are our *own* worst enemies. The sole reason for avoiding negative thoughts is that they have an uncanny way of becoming self-fulfilling prophecies. Hardly a golfer alive has not experienced this phenomenon. It's telling yourself *not* to hit it into the water, *not* to slice it into the big elm on the right side of the fairway, *not* to top a three wood by pulling your head up at the last minute, *not* to move your hands and arms awkwardly in the middle of your swing—*not, not, not!* Negative thoughts can ruin a decent swing. They can ruin a *half*-decent swing. If we are going to play a half-decent round of golf, never mind playing *bogey* golf, we must attack the game with a positive attitude by using positive thoughts and expecting positive outcomes—or at the very least, avoiding negative ones.

This is not rocket science, brain surgery, or quantum mechanics. Even under the best of circumstances, even when you're playing lights out, things can go wrong in an instant. The wheels can come off the wagon without any provocation at all. It happens to all of us: beginners, bogey golfers, scratch golfers, and even Masters champions. Think again about poor Phil Mickelson's last hole in the 2006 U.S. Open at Winged Foot, the one referred to in Chapter 4. If you happened to see that round or the countless replays for days afterward, you'll have no trouble calling up the image of the quizzical expression on Mickelson's face, nor will you ever forget him burying his head in his hands after hitting the courtesy tent on 18 in Sunday's final round and blowing a sure championship. It doesn't take much to upset the fragile balance in a good round of golf. My point is that practicing positive thinking is as critical to your success as practicing correct techniques.

If you have trouble with this, it may be necessary for you to do some creative visualization. The best experience I ever had in my fifty years of playing tennis was the day I got good and sick of beating myself, so I just imagined a judgmental and very hypercritical self being banished from the court. I did this right in the middle of a set in which I was losing badly. I pictured myself telling him to get the hell out, and then I imagined him picking up his gear and trudging slowly toward the exit and leaving the indoor facility in which I was playing. Not only did I play much better after that, I actually turned things around enough to win the match. Visualize a critical self being booed off the course. Visualize a situation in which the mind *only* knows positive language, can make *only* positive, or at least constructive comments during the round. Visualize your inner judge doing The Inner Judge Trudge—down the fairway, across a tee box or two, out to the parking lot, into his or her car, and slowly driving away.

If you have to work at this, you should work at this!

Yogi Berra can't say it any better.

If you want to avoid letting yourself get into your own head (or your kitchen), it follows that it's just as important not to let someone *else* get in there, either. It's hard enough keeping your *self* out of your head when the situation demands it. Play golf with a bravado that dares anything and anyone to try to get into your head. This will probably take a fair amount of disciplined practice, and you have to believe in it. It is just as critical to practice this mental skill as it is to practice the physical skills the game requires. When you are making your shot, make your head off limits—to everything. Clear the mechanism, and keep it clear until the ball is safely on its way toward the target.

One of the best ways to practice this is to play alone. I remember several of my solo rounds during that first summer very well. Frequently, I entered into a dialogue with myself which I found calming—as long as I was *not* playing Judge or

Critic or Mr. Hyde (see Chapter 9) to myself. Keep the process to—and within—yourself. This is one of the truly magnificent aspects of the sport, different from almost every other sport that involves a ball. You can establish a relationship with anything on the course—the birds, the sky, the grass, your ball, your seven iron—or with nothing. Try to see yourself as part of the larger landscape, or even the cosmos. You can also establish a relationship with yourself that, given enough room in which to grow and develop, can become much more than just internal companionship. It can become a buffer between you and the distractions of competition, friendly or formal. It can become an antidote to some of the more perplexing dilemmas of your life away from the golf course. It can allow you to dream, yet "not make dreams your master."

Thank you, Mr. Kipling!

Chapter Eight
"Am I Really Just a Hack?"

> Don't, no don't sink the boat
> That you built, that you built to keep afloat.
> Flogging Molly

> Always keep in mind that if God didn't
> want a man to have mulligans, golf balls
> wouldn't come three to a sleeve.
> Dan Jenkins

I've lost count of how often my IPP and I look at each other after a bad shot, and one of us will say in disgust, "What a couple of hacks!" And then the other guy says with even more conviction, "Really!" It doesn't take much to provoke an exchange like this. That is probably because, like most golfers, we keep expecting more from ourselves, which is a good thing provided we can keep the expectations grounded, if not limited (see Chapter 15).

In the summer of 2006, we played more than a hundred rounds. It was our first summer with season passes, and we wanted to squeeze every last round we could out of them. I'm sure there were a few golfers who played more frequently, but we got our licks in. It was a terrific summer because we hardly ever got rained out, it was never too hot to play, and our schedules meshed perfectly for most of the summer. I was on summer vacation, and my IPP works nights.

We had one serious problem, though: we weren't improving.

But so what? We were having fun, and we weren't getting any worse. So who cares? Maybe we're just hacks. Hacks have fun, they can get around the course fairly well, they rarely hold up the group behind them. So what? What's so bad about being a hack?

Before I continue, we must agree on the definition of a "hack." In dictionary language, a hack is a noun: one accustomed to "working for hire esp. with loose or easy professional standards." It can also be a verb: "to cut or reshape by or as if by crude or ruthless strokes." It pains me to recall how often there have been whole rounds, let alone individual strokes, in which **both** of these definitions were true. Hard as it is to keep my chin up during times like that, I keep coming back to the game, as do, I am quite certain, most of those who play.

What, then, are we to do about this most cruel paradox. We are hacks who still aspire to play bogey golf? Apart from adopting the practice of just grinning and bearing it or spending your life's savings on lessons, there may be a third option which comes down to asserting to any and all, with Nixonian conviction, "I am not a hack!" Over time, that single proclamation can become quite reassuring, but it takes more than just semantic manipulation to transform it from a bad case of false advertising to a vital and fully actualized personal manifesto.

One morning in my second summer, bogey golf was still a country mile away from the flatlands I was playing on. I was a permanent resident in the Kingdom of Golf Hackdom (KGH, from here on). I started thinking too much. I desperately wanted to determine once and for all what the expression "hack" meant exactly and whether I fit the definition. Call it self-absorption, narcissism, or obsession … whatever. I began to dissect this self-inflicted, offensive slam in order to save some face when my game started falling apart. I wanted to make certain that I was at least a cut or two above a common hack, a casual golfer with some of Mr. Webster's "loose or easy professional standards."

There are plenty of true hacks out there playing golf. Furthermore, most of them would probably freely, proudly admit to such a categorization. They're the smart ones! Happy hacks can often play well over their heads from time to time, and still be just as happy when they're *not* playing over their heads. They know they don't play often enough to merit being at any other level than right there in the KGH. They don't go out on the range regularly to work on their game, they tend not to take lessons, they play irregularly, and they don't come unglued when their score exceeds 100. For any number of reasons, when they do play, they don't care what the result is; they just want to have fun.

> *If they do care, they will eventually do something about it.*

To get a better handle on this concept, imagine the classic bell-shaped curve. Drop a perpendicular line through a point about one-third of the way up the left slope of the curve and drop another one through a point about one-third of the way up the right slope of the curve. Delete, remove, or erase the two separate thirds on the ends. In your mind, can you picture the big hump in the middle now? The original bell-shaped curve minus its nose and its tail. You've identified the golfers who are either eligible for or already imprisoned, by choice or necessity, in the KGH.

You have just separated the true beginners (the left third) and the true believers (the right third) from the rest of us commoners, among whom are a healthy number aspiring to play bogey golf. We are a large percentage of the playing public. We're in this together, and we're in it for the long haul

… we need to stay focused on the goal until I can get us all out of the KGH alive.

Suppose, then, that you want to make a jump from that midsection of the bell curve to the right hand segment. You have no pretensions of becoming a pro, and you doubt seriously that you'll play tournaments. You may not quite reach bogey golf either, but it is the desire, the commitment, and the resolve to stop playing like a hack—and stop feeling like one—that drives you to want to make the jump. You just want to be a true believer, a legitimate non-hack, to play with a certain amount of dignity. The first thing to do (perhaps the only thing to do) is to forgive yourself, to relax about a few things. It's time to examine some of the finer points of the KGH in order to see where we can let ourselves off the hook and where we can't.

Advancing the Ball

It might be well to consider that if you have advanced the ball, you have done enough to elevate yourself out of the KGH. Advancing the ball is, indeed, a large part of the game of golf, but we shouldn't just settle for that. It is much better than making it go sideways or backward, certainly, but sometimes it doesn't go far enough forward. In order to earn an exemption from having to enroll in the KGH's own version of Qualifying School, we must do the following *five* things in addition to simply advancing the ball:

> 1. Make the ball go in the general direction of the green.
>
> 2. Satisfy ourselves with the distance the ball travels, even if it's a bit off line;

3. Commit to the club selection and to getting the ball to do what we expect it do;

4. Do whatever it takes physically *and* mentally to *recover* after a mis-hit or a wasted shot;

5. Keep firmly in mind a simple truth: We cannot hit a good shot when we are either angry or rushed.

If that sounds too harsh, there's a fair amount of wiggle room in these five rules, so you have to be fair to yourself. Remember this, though: you can't be fair to yourself if you're not honest with yourself first. This means understanding your permanent limitations, understanding your temporary limitations, understanding the limitations of the course and the weather, and finally, understanding whether or not you can let yourself off the hook based on any of the above understandings. Escaping the KGH means finding the middle ground between not being able to forgive yourself and not taking the game seriously enough.

Now, I know I am straying somewhat from the simple idea of advancing the ball here, but being able to let yourself off the hook on a more-or-less regular basis involves a number of factors, and I haven't even tackled the hardest one of all—expectations (see Chapter 15). As for advancing the ball, it's basically a judgment call. You're not a hack if you're advancing the ball toward the green, even if the ball wanders a bit on the way. Playing bogey golf is easy enough to do even if the ball does *not* always go in a straight line from the tee to the flag stick provided that you *not* allow self-incriminating sorts of demons to sabotage your play.

Two more tips emerge from the list of five items above. They

are formulas more than they are tips; one is for distance
assessment and one is for recovery assessment.

Formula 1—Distance Assessment for Irons

Call your pitching wedge a ten iron, and
assume that a wedge shot can cover distances
anywhere from roughly ten yards to about one
hundred yards; move "up" a club (down in
club number) for every ten yards of distance
farther from the pin as shown in this formula:

ten iron	= 10—100 yards
nine iron	= 100—110 yards
eight iron	= 110—120 yards
seven iron	= 120—130 yards
six iron	= 130—140 yards
five iron	= 140—150 yards
four iron	= 150—160 yards
three iron	= 160—170 yards
two iron	= 170—180 yards

This formula is merely a set of approximate distances to start
with if you do not already have such a formula of your own.
Your distances will vary widely depending on how often
you play, what your club speed is, your upper body strength,
experience, equipment, and about fifty other factors, so adjust
these distances for yourself in any way you need to. And,
of course, the more experience and command of your game
you have, the more restrictive and specific these distance
estimates become. The point here is that the more certain you
can be about your own distances, the more capable you are of
assessing the requirements for your shots.

Formula 2—Recovery

Mis-hitting a ball or wasting a shot now and then should not, by itself, be capable of ruining a round. What *will* ruin a round is taking several more unnecessary shots to recover from one of those mistakes.

Ideally, recovery from a bad shot should cost you only one extra stroke. In other words, a mis-hit or a wasted shot should add only one stroke to your score: you make the mistake, and then you pay the price using one and only one extra stroke to get back approximately to where you should have been in the first place had you made a good shot.

Perfection is for golfers who shoot par. Bogey golfers need to focus on minimizing the negative effect of *major* mistakes. If you waste a shot or mis-hit one, take a deep breath, take a new look at the target, and get back in the game. Remember, if bogey golf is your objective, and you add two recovery shots to your score on a certain hole, that's two pars you have to earn to make up for the mistake. Each time this happens, think carefully about what you need to do and how you need to do it so that recovery becomes a relatively methodical part of your game, a simple matter for you when, *not if*, it becomes necessary.

"Am I Really Just a Hack?"

Mis-hits

If you know how to play golf, and you play relatively frequently, you should slowly but surely be reducing the number of mis-hits in your game. Mis-hits occur for two main reasons: lack of skill and lack of focus. Both can be remedied by lessons, practice, concentration, repetition, practice, video taping, practice, slowing down your takeaway … and, yes, practice. I usually try to count my mis-hits per round, and if I get past five, I consider it a bad round. I don't quit playing when I hit five because I try to remain hopeful that change is just around the corner. I also am not above using the rest of a bad round as a practice round and, if I can, forgetting about the score. I know the difference between a mis-hit and a good hit. For the most part, one mis-hit should only require one extra stroke … if you work hard. Usually, though, it isn't even that favorable because, as often as not, a mis-hit produces more mis-hits. As far as I know, no one has yet figured out why, but it has something to do with a sort of insidious predisposition toward repetition that occurs within The Dark Side of our brains. It's the part that makes your body an unsuspecting and unwitting accomplice in a comedy of errors. To break the chain, get back on track, regroup, not fall prey to The Dark Side—whatever—you have to be careful not to make a mis-hit worse by taking it either too lightly or too seriously, and allowing it to spawn more of its kind. It's good to avoid mis-hitting the ball, but if you *are* mis-hitting the ball, it's good to be doing so less and less as the rounds (and years) go by. If you cannot do this, then you will doubtless earn yourself a permanent home in the KGH.

Wasted Shots

Wasted shots are not the same thing as mis-hits. I am still trying to get the distinction clear in my own mind. You can mis-hit a ball, and the hole can still be salvaged. A mis-hit might be simply a matter of a slight miscalculation that takes the ball off line a bit, or in the case of a putt, sends the ball too far past the hole or leaves it just a bit too short. A wasted shot is a total loss. It's a shot that might have been topped, sculled, scuffed, stubbed, bladed, or scooped. It might be even a whiff, or you might have hit a tree that could easily have been avoided. Wasted shots are usually the result of not enough concentration, laziness, or out-and-out carelessness. It's usually a shot conceived within who-knows-what corner of The Dark Side. It can leave you wondering, as Colin Montgomerie wondered aloud, "What shot was *that?*" when his wayward seven iron shot into the rough on the eighteenth hole of the final round at the 2006 U.S. Open cost him at least a share of the lead, if not the championship outright.

For those of us working hard to exit the KGH, wasting a shot should be completely avoidable. Mis-hitting a shot is unavoidable from time to time, especially if you are working on your swing, or trying out a new grip, or any one of a thousand simple little things that we do to try to improve. Wasted shots happen when there has been too little thought *prior* to the shot or too much thought *during* the shot. They are born in our bad habits, and they can occur at every spot on the course, from tee to green. The more you play, the more you will become familiar with the difference.

Mis-hitting the ball does not necessarily mean that your score will be negatively affected, but a wasted shot definitely means that you will have to take at least one and very likely two or more extra strokes on the hole. While I try very hard not to exceed five mis-hits, I am much less generous when it comes to wasted shots because, again, they're completely avoidable if I am being mindful (see Chapter 2) when I play. Work hard to eliminate wasted shots. If you can't at least reduce their number over time, bogey golf is probably not going to happen for you. Let's say that your goal is to score in the low 90s for eighteen holes. If you keep the total number of wasted shots and mis-hits below ten, and your handicap is, let's say 20, your adjusted score is going to be very respectable. To be more specific, assume that par for the golf course you are playing is 72, and your handicap is 20. To make par in an event where your handicap is going to be figured in, you need to shoot 92. Say you *would* have shot exactly bogey golf, a 90, except for ten wasted shots and mis-hits. That gives you a total score of 100. Adjusted for your handicap, you shot an 80. *An 80!* Not bad. It won't win tournaments, but you're in the hunt, at least.

Okay, take away all ten of those wasted shots just for the heck of it. Now —

> *a) you shot a natural bogey round, and*

> *b) adjusted for your handicap, you shot a 70.*

That score *will* win you some tournaments, or some rounds, or at least some free drinks. It will also start lowering your handicap. The cost for mis-hitting a ball or wasting a shot comes in the shot (or shots) that you absolutely must now make in order to salvage the hole. So here is the second "A-ha! moment" I'd like to share with you:

Do whatever you must do, mentally and physically, to keep the number of strokes it takes to recover from a bad shot as close to one as possible.

It never hurts to reflect on how to avoid wasting a shot. Wasted shots qualify you immediately for entry into the KGH. It is discouraging that correcting the wasting of shots is devilishly difficult. The good news is that when you have whittled down your wasted shots sufficiently, you are not only

guaranteed *not* to have to stay in the KGH, but you also get
the pleasure of getting closer to bogey golf. I remember very
clearly the first time I broke 50 for nine holes, and I remember
very clearly the day I played a single ball for an entire eighteen
holes. These were memorable because I was struggling to gain
some self-respect on the golf course. However, I remember the
very few times I have played bogey golf much more clearly,
and I am here to tell you that you don't have to do it every
time you play to feel successful. Having bogey golf as a goal
is a perfect objective for lunch-pail golfers who don't get to
play all the time or who don't have unlimited practice balls,
sponsors, or a golden parachute.

In Chapter 7, I discussed giving your head a little bit of time
off often enough in a round so that your muscle memory,
your natural ability, and your focus get some exercise without
obstruction. I must caution you, however, that if you do *not*
use your head when the situation demands it, you will rarely,
if ever, make lasting progress.

Avoiding wasted shots means *not* doing one or more of the
following (list alert!) on every shot depending on where you
are on the course:

* taking chances;
* over-swinging in order to get miles and miles down the fairway;
* gripping the club too tightly or "trying too hard" during your swing;
* thinking so much about what you are doing that you get in your own way;
* trying to get it all back after one wasted shot or a mis-hit;
* peeking too soon after the shot;

* saying "I'm gonna kill it!" on your drive;
* trying to carry the creek when you should be laying up;
* pretending to be a professional when you're an amateur;
* forgetting to read the green as carefully as time permits before you putt;
* forgetting to keep your mind clear, head still, and body in control;
* thinking about work, home, people, your score, your partner's score, or come-what-may shooting par;
* suddenly, halfway through your swing, twitching your hands, elbows, arms, or fingers trying to compensate for what suddenly feels like an incorrect swing;
* forgetting to strive for definite rhythm and fluidity in your swing;
* forgetting about tempo and timing;
* jerking or flexing just as you hit the ball;
* being afraid to stop in mid-swing when something about the swing doesn't feel right;
* failing to let the club do the work;
* losing your balance during the swing;
* guiding or steering your shot;
* letting bad luck, bad weather, or bad play incubate your victim mentality;
* forgetting to commit to the target, the club, and the swing;
* thinking that because the tree, the lake, or the Port-O-Potty is there, you *have to avoid it at all costs*.

CHAPTER EIGHT

As often as I might play like a hack, I am reasonably certain, now, that I am not one. I realized a few seasons ago that I would not be satisfied staying at that level, so I have tried to take some steps to keep that from happening. I could do more, for sure. It's hard to play golf even halfway seriously without wanting to get better. Though it was frustrating not to lower my handicap a bit last summer, I recall many exciting and fulfilling moments when I felt like a real bogey golfer. All that really means is that I take nine extra shots per every nine holes. That has become The Gold Standard in determining whether I remain a prisoner in the KGH or make good on a successful prison break to chase bogey.

An Afterthought About Your Grip

Among the most important decisions you'll have to make before getting serious about chasing bogey is what kind of grip you want to use. When I finally discovered that I needed to make that decision—and then went with a choice no matter how uncomfortable it felt at first—I had taken a huge step away from the KGH. Huge.

As most Golf for Dummies clones will tell you, there are two grips to choose from, the interlocking grip and the overlapping grip. You can probably invent your own, but why bother. Think of all the research that has been done on this, and think of how it has been whittled down to two basic grips. Why bother reinventing the wheel? Try both and then choose one. It's that simple. In my second summer of playing, I chose the interlocking grip, and it didn't take me more than a month to feel totally comfortable with it.

You will most likely need to use a different grip for putting. There are a few more choices on the putting green than in the tee box and on the fairway, and it's critical to experiment

"Am I Really Just a Hack?"

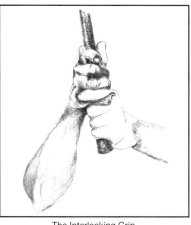

The Interlocking Grip

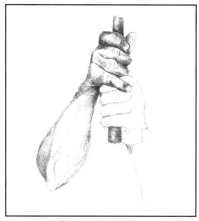

The Overlapping Grip

with the options before making your choice. There are plenty of books, videos, late night television shows on the Golf Channel, not to mention lessons with your local golf pro, so you should not lack for information about the options. After two seasons of lackluster putting, I did some reading and discovered something called the cross-hand grip. The theory behind this grip is that placing the left (front) hand below the right or dominant hand gives the whole putting mechanism more stability because you can lock the wrist and make it an extension of the putter.

Though there may be little adjustments you'll make in your grips from time to time, having a grip of your own is one of golf's simplest and most reliable security systems.

CHAPTER NINE
GOT SLICE?

As I teed the ball up again I settled into a
feeling of stomach and hips, making a center
there for my swing. And then a vivid image
appeared in my mind's eye, of a turquoise
ball traveling down the right side of the
fairway with a tail hook toward the green.
I took my stance and waggled the club
carefully, aware that the image of the shot
was incredibly vivid. Then I swung and the
ball followed the path laid down in my mind.

Michael Murphy

I'm not saying my golf game went bad,
but if I grew tomatoes, they'd come up
sliced.

Miller Barber,
Lee Trevino

Once, several summers ago, long after I should have known
better, my IPP and I stood on the first tee on The Lakes Nine
early in the season. It's a beautiful, rather haunting 370-yard
hole that stretches down a fairly steep and narrow hillside,
widens a bit, then bends just enough to the right so that
the green is not quite visible from the tee. The flagstick's
invisibility is due as much to the dense woods on the right
side of the fairway as it is to the dogleg to the right, and there
is an equally dense wooded area all along the left side of the
fairway. The most tantalizing feature of the first half of the
hole is a narrow creek slanting all the way across the fairway

about 235 yards from the tee box. That creek just stands out there daring unsuspecting aspirants to try to put their drives across it—even if only on the bounce. Every season I give it a few tries. I have not succeeded yet, but I know I will someday, because this hole sets up perfectly for what will some season soon be a fade rather than a slice. On that particular morning, after my IPP had put his drive right down the middle so that it came to rest within a foot of the gleaming white 150-yard stake on the near side of the creek, I decided it was one of those mornings. Four drives later, I changed my mind.

Four good Top Flights into the woods. Every shot went *way* right. My IPP was sympathetic, then incredulous, and finally doubled over at the amazing show of repetitive ineptitude he was witnessing. The first two drives were such exact duplicates of each other that I am certain they hit the same tree. Two "THOCK" sounds deep in the forest were all the evidence I needed to draw that sickening conclusion. The third drive, though it was somewhat less deep into the woods and traveled farther, whipped through so many leafy surfaces that it sounded like a heat-seeking missile high up in the canopy. The fourth drive, for which I prepared longer and considered more deeply (regrettably) reflected all the worst consequences of thinking too much before making a shot. It was not only sliced but topped as well. In less than a split second after impact it ricocheted off the cart path fewer than fifty yards beyond the tee box and headed straightaway into the woods at tree trunk level in search of its predecessors. I vowed then and there to begin working on reducing and ultimately eliminating my slice—thus joining ninety percent of the rest of the would-be bogey golfers in the world. I began to understand why I keep hearing radio ads for subscriptions to *Golf Digest* exhorting listeners to "Act Now! in order to receive ('While supplies last!') a promotional video tape called 'Cure Your Slice Now!'" Funny thing, though. I ordered the magazine subscription, and waited and waited for that damn video, and it never came. Needless to say, I did not renew the subscription. I did, however, keep my slice.

Now—at this point, I have to say again that I am *not* a pro. You can and should take anything and everything I say here that sounds remotely like "Technical Tips for Improving Your Game" with a grain of salt. In fact, you should check it out with your own local pro—or maybe you *did* receive that video, and you can check it against that, too! Go with the proven professionals first, then add this to your stash if it helps. I am not trying to pass myself off as a slice expert, but I can tell you this: while making friends with your putter is a critical step to reaching the level of bogey golf, being able to hit a reasonably straight drive is probably in second place. It will keep you playing the game, so for what it's worth, figure out how *not* to hit your ball into the woods (let alone *four* balls). Here, then, in stripped down and decidedly nontechnical language, are a few things you need to come to terms with if you're trying not to hit your ball into the woods, or the water, or some pleasantly inviting border area just beyond a sign that reads, "Private: No Looking for Balls Beyond This Sign."

1. The reason the ball curves, whether sharply or gently, is that you are coming across the ball at an angle instead of hitting it square. The object is to try to make the club face be perpendicular to the target line when it strikes the ball. If you can do this already, you may not need 2–11 below.

2. You need to have—and keep—the target in mind. You're NOT aiming at the woods (or whatever) on the right.

3. You must not fall away from your drive. Pay attention to what your body looks *and* feels like after you finish your follow-through.

4. Finish high. *Do not finish around behind and leaning back*. See 8 below.

5. Your grip and stance directly affects the straightness of your drive, so experiment with where your right thumb is when you grip your driver, and experiment with how open your stance is when you address the ball on the tee. Play around with some slight variations in where your front foot is. These things wind up playing a fairly critical role in your success driving off the tee.

6. The most mysterious and unpredictable part of any golf swing involves understanding the whole issue of what golf instructors refer to as "the plane." I will try to make this as simple as I can. You want to keep the plane your driver travels along as two dimensional as possible, and you want to do it as consistently as possible. It does not happen naturally by itself, nor does it happen overnight. I suppose this is why good golfers spend as much time as they do on the driving range. Many instructors use videotaping as a way of seeing what kind of plane your swings are in.

7. Often, after you've hit your drive, you can look down where the tee still is—or used to be—and see a mark in the turf where your club head scuffed through the topsoil. If you have a slice, and you're a right-handed golfer, you'll see a definite cross-wise mark, with the "grain" moving from upper right to lower left as you look down while you're still in your stance. The angle can often be as much as 45 degrees. Here's the proof that you are coming across the ball, giving it a good deal of sideways spin and directing it on an off-center, curved path. This is the way baseball pitchers put

spin on their curve balls, but remember that they do it intentionally.

8. Back to 4 above. Focus on where your hands and wrists are at the end of your follow-through. If they are down by your shoulder, chances are good that you are coming across the ball. Keep telling yourself this: "Finish high, finish high" and there's a good chance that your slice will begin to lessen in sharpness. Your hands and wrists should finish somewhere up near and behind your head. This is not baseball, softball, tennis, or weed-whacking.

9. Keep your balance. Shift as much weight as you can to your front leg without losing your balance. This takes a *lot* of practice and repetition. Watch a video or a live tournament, and memorize what a good swing looks like.

10. On the same subject, feel the *forward* motion of your body and of your club as you make contact. Your weight should be moving in the direction of your target. If your mind focuses on the target, it is easier for your body to do the same thing. When I watch other golfers on the course, I try to see if the rotation of their bodies is in a narrow cylinder, only as wide as the distance from their butts to where the ball was teed up. I check to make sure their whole body moves *forward* toward the target as the swing happens.

11. Occasionally, I read or hear the phrase "Stand tall to the ball," and it is helpful advice. Even though your back is supposed to be slightly bent at the waist (and straight!) over the ball, and your knees are, too, stand tall to the ball. Even though your head is tilted forward—over

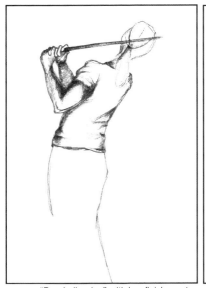

"Baseball swing" with low finish creates slices - or worse. Finish high!

Wrists must be at head level, elbows at shoulder level on follow through.

the ball and looking down—feel tall over the ball. Even though your stance may be somewhat wide (although your feet should be about as far apart as your shoulders and not much more), stand tall to the ball. Even though you may be playing horribly, don't quit on standing tall to the ball.

12. Finally, here is one of *the* most important jobs to remember, practice, and be conscious of: *make certain that you bring your right (outside) hip all the way through as you complete your swing. In addition, it helps immeasurably if you are conscious of your right elbow staying as close to your body as possible without hitting it.*

I've taken exactly two lessons in my short career as a bogey golfer hopeful, and I can assure you that not every lesson is a good lesson. So far, I'm batting .500 on lessons. The first lesson I had, I watched the guy hit almost all of the balls in my bucket before he finally said "Now you hit a few." He assumed, I suppose, that I would learn best by watching him, and I know there's truth to that because I do watch and learn. But, come on! The more he hit, the more I felt like this lesson was about him, not me. The only reason I have forgiven him is because I learned something from him that I have not forgotten since, and that is that I prefer to cock or hinge my wrists *before* the so-called "takeaway" (bringing the club steadily back to a position high up over your head and parallel to the ground) rather than during it. It's one less thing to do once you begin your swing.

I bring this up for two reasons. The first one has to do with believing that no matter how ineffective a lesson might be for you, there are going to be at least a few things you can hang onto. In fact, you should approach every experience in this game with that attitude. Then, when all hell's breaking loose for you on the course, you can be like Pollyanna, telling yourself again and again that not only is everything going to be all right, but by golly, you found new success with your lob wedge, or you made a good fairway wood shot, or you didn't lose any balls, or it's just so doggone *nice* outside! Get my drift?

Try taking a lesson, and look for even the smallest tidbit of good advice, or the most specific of generic tips, as your instructor works on your game. Note: If you *do* take a lesson, make sure you tell the pro exactly what you want to work on before you start—and stick to your guns. I remember my first lesson where I allowed the guy to run roughshod all over me starting with about a fifteen-minute lecture on the history of the game and what hitting a golf ball is all about, the physics and the chemistry and all that torque and forward motion jargon. Maybe he thought I was hoping to make it to the PGA Tour that same summer, and he wanted to front-load my lesson with as much information as he could. I distinctly remember wondering who had put what into this guy's orange juice. I just wanted to fix my slice. He was too impressed with himself for that, and even after I told him what I wanted to work on, he just kind of launched into this whole "Step back for a moment, Grasshopper. What do we want to do in golf? What's our main objective" kind of schtick. Luckily for the pro shop, he moved on shortly afterward, and I never saw him again. Now that my cynicism has waned, maybe this season, I'll take another one.

The second reason I mention my first lesson is so I can emphasize that cocking my wrists early on in the whole swing guarantees that my club face will at least approximate, if not duplicate, the intimate relationship it had when I first addressed the ball. I want that club face to be perpendicular to the target line at contact. So cocking my wrist during address helps me feel more like I am sort of ghosting the point of impact before I have even begun my takeaway. This sets it in my mind; it feels very natural to do it this way now. Golf is tailormade for an anal retentive person, one who absolutely loves repeatability. The trick, of course, is to make sure you're dumping bad habits and replacing them with good ones, whether you're in the tee box or on the green. I guess I have to emphasize here that the only way to develop some of these habits is to practice — somewhere, anywhere. My IPP is still way better at this than I am; he practices on the living room rug, and his efforts on behalf of an improved swing have made a bare spot where you can just see the threads now, no color or texture. I call him up sometimes in the middle of winter when my golf clubs are buried under winter clothes out in the vestibule, and I'll eventually get around to mentioning something about the upcoming golf season, and before I've even finished my sentence, he'll say, "I've got my seven iron in my hands right now, Fitz!" He's probably going to play regular bogey golf long before I do ... but I'm going to claim that I taught him everything he knows.

Let's go back out onto the first tee on the Lakes Nine for a moment. I have about five or six spots on the course where I love to stand and just think of the possibilities. I suppose it is natural for the first tee on a course you play over and over again to be one of those spots, but I would choose *this* tee on the Lakes Nine over the first tee on the front nine and the tenth tee on the back nine hands down. The mystery of the green, way down there past the creek and around the bend, the lure of the creek itself—just close enough to encourage dreaming, the corridor-like feeling of the woods on both sides, my history here ... I love it.

I tee my ball up and take several gentle practice swings and think about how still I am going to keep my head and how fluidly I am going to swing the driver. I look down the fairway, and I pick out a spot somewhere on the plateau that is just in front of the grassy line that is the bank of the creek. I shut out the almost overwhelming desire to "kill it" and carry the creek at last. I am going to settle for smooth and straight. I'm going to feel the swing develop slowly during the takeaway, and I want to feel a gradually increasing momentum bringing the driver down through the ball as I look at it intently. I'll see where the ball was. I am going to follow through as far around and as high up as I can, and I'll look up only when my shoulders and back won't let my head stay down any longer. I will feel my hands comfortably gripped around the shaft of the driver and sense their presence right up behind my head.

I will only hit one ball, and I will not hear any loud "THOCK" in the woods. It won't matter to me that I am still on the near side of the creek because I know I can hit a nice little seven iron to the green. We will stroll easily down the cart path talking about the Twins game last night or the warmth of the day or how fine it would be to birdie this hole. Yes, this hole is moving steadily up through the ranks of favored holes on the course. Maybe, in several different ways, it will be number one by the end of this season. I look forward to that.

CHAPTER TEN
THE MOST IMPORTANT SPLIT SECOND IN GOLF

The challenging but scenic par 5 second hole on the Lakes Nine at Lester Park Golf Course with the mythic spruce guarding access to the green.   Photograph by Diane Hilden

> You can spend a lifetime, and, if you're honest with yourself, never once was your work perfect.
> Charlton Heston

> Thinking instead of acting is the number one golf disease.
> Sam Snead

After seven seasons of playing, I have finally figured out exactly which split second of every single stroke will make the most difference in whether that stroke has a chance to be a memorable one—memorable, that is, for the *right* reasons. When I play a round of golf with someone else, my IPP or anyone else, we use a whole array of adjectives to describe good shots, all of which feel satisfying and affirming for a person with ambitions of playing bogey golf. These adjectives include (but are not limited to) decent, acceptable, workable, workmanlike, respectable, playable, elegant, majestic, phenomenal, good, and great. Note: I intentionally refrain from using the word *"perfect"* because a good (any one of the adjectives listed above may here be substituted for "good") shot can be a long way from "perfect" and still be successful. Sometimes it can even be extraordinarily pleasing. A perfect shot can happen, of course, but it's a good idea to avoid *expecting* a perfect shot. The material in this chapter relates very closely to what Chapter 15 will deal with because I have learned painfully and arduously that expecting perfection is the death knell not only of playing bogey golf but of enjoying oneself on the course at all. At this point, I can imagine even moderately competitive players interrupting me right here and asking if I am not, once again, encouraging you to settle for mediocrity. The short answer is a resounding *"No,"* but I should respond briefly to that worry before I move on to discuss this chapter's primary focus.

I like perfection as much as anyone. I can honestly say that I have hit enough shots that I could justifiably call "perfect" to know that perfection happens—rarely, but it happens. In my very first summer, I was standing over my ball less than fifty yards from the green on the second hole of the Lakes Nine at Lester Park Golf Course. My ball was on a steep downhill slope about thirty yards from the green. A towering forty-five-foot spruce was directly between my ball and the flagstick. I knew I needed loft much more than I needed distance, so I pulled my pitching wedge from my bag and just kept telling myself, "Keep your head down and swing through, keep your head down, and swing through." At that point in my golfing career, I hadn't started practicing how to use a pitching wedge, so I was really flying blind. Somehow, though, I managed to do the right thing, and the ball arched beautifully right up and over the very top of the spruce and plunked right down on the green. It was, in a word, perfect. Like most casual golfers and their references to shots that keep them coming back to the game in spite of the frustration and angst they must suffer through, that memorable wedge shot was worth every miserable shot it took me to get to it. I remember the shot every time I walk past that spruce.

A different sort of perfect shot was a long putt I hit two summers later. I was playing the sixth hole of the same nine-hole course, the Lakes Nine, late one lazy July afternoon. The putting green slopes gently back down toward the fairway from the flag. I had hit a pretty decent nine iron a bit too strongly causing the ball to roll way past the pin which was positioned at the front of the green. The ball came to rest about three yards off the green at the very back. As I stood alone quietly looking at the distance this putt would have to travel, a huge thousand-footer came into view out on the lake. I watched it for a few minutes marveling at its length and its purposefulness as it surged away from the harbor.

Back to my shot, I was tempted to hit a seven iron bump-and-run shot, but I knew I couldn't hit that shot softly enough to keep the ball from rolling back off the green on the downhill side, so I opted for the putter. I laughed to myself as I was lining it up, because I had never sunk a putt that long before in my life from *on* the green, and here I was rather significantly *off* the green. I hit the ball as close to full tilt as I dared, and it rolled gracefully all the way across the green and fell right into the cup with the flagstick still in place. I was stunned. I did not try to fool myself with the classic "just the way I planned it" line. I knew that I had barely even hoped it would go in, let alone planned that it would. I paced it off carefully: fifty-two

A Canadian "laker" heads toward Duluth Harbor to load coal
behind the first and ninth fairways at Lester Park Golf Course.
Photograph by Diane Hilden

feet. Another entry in my own personal shot scrapbook, the one entitled, *No One's Going to Believe THIS One.* Serendipitous, yes, and perfect.

And that's my point. At our level of play, it's important not to use a standard of perfection that only pros use, nor to expect perfection from yourself for two simple reasons: 1) the disappointment (or anger) that follows failure, and 2) the pure joy (or ecstasy) that follows perfection.

I do not pretend to expect perfection from myself because I know that perfection is for perfectionists. Professional golfers must be perfectionists. Fortunately or unfortunately, that trait is not part of my arsenal or skill set, and it is not needed for bogey golf. I realized very quickly that I cannot expect perfection unless I am willing to spend much more cash and much more time working on my game. That is just not possible, and I am not even certain that it's desirable. I am very happy, at this point, taking perfection on its own terms. It happens from time to time, but the odds of it happening when

I *expect* it to happen are small, even negligible. I will not stop trying for it, but I don't let myself expect it.

Now—back to the topic of this chapter. To repeat: I know the precise split second at which a good shot can be born, when a bad shot can be avoided, and when a *perfect* shot has an outside chance of being conceived, even if it is not realized.

> *It is the split-second immediately after your club makes contact with the ball.*

The bottom line is this: your shot is going to be fine if your eyes are on the ball and your head is perfectly still when the club head meets the ball, pushes through it, and sends it on its way. By now, it has probably become quite apparent to you that these split seconds do not last nearly as long as their after-effects do, whether they are positive or negative.

That's the most important split second in golf: *not* the instant of impact, but the split second right *after* that instant when you either keep your head down and your eye on the place where the ball was just a moment ago, or lift it up too early to peek at the path of your ball.

Somehow, (the video taping that many golf instructors offer their students can probably show this to you) when your head moves even slightly, even just *after* the club makes contact, the path of the ball in the air, or its path on the green, can be adversely affected. There is a very good reason why we can see countless examples of this simple rule of thumb in action when we watch golf on television. Professional golfers seem to make this split second an unconscious and automatic part of their routine. It doesn't just happen in the tee box, either. It is just as noticeable on the putting green. If you're a visual learner, if you know how to do most of your sports-related moves because you've watched people do them either live or on television, you should be able to teach yourself about this split second just by watching a few tournaments. Here's a beautiful example:

March 17, 2007 — St. Patrick's Day — A Lesson on the Green!

I am watching a golf lesson right now. It's taking place at the 2007 Arnold Palmer Bay Hill Classic in Orlando, Florida. Paul Casey from England and Rocco Mediate from Western Pennsylvania are tied for the lead at eight under par in the third round. On the tenth green, they both just putted from a distance of not more than eight feet from the cup, and they both missed the hole by less than half an inch. I watched their heads. It was not just my imagination when I saw them each look toward the hole just as their putters hit the ball. It was a sort of fluid motion all in the same moment … *take the putter back and then slowly bring it toward the ball accelerating through impact, and the head instantaneously follows the putter in the direction of the hole on the follow through*. I continued to watch these guys as well as the small knot of golfers chasing them and they all did the same thing putt after putt. They narrowly missed the cup on quite a high number of putts.

Minutes (and commercials) pass. Now, I'm watching another lesson, same tournament, different player—the world's best. Tiger Woods is on 17; he has about a ten-foot putt. The camera zooms in on his grip … gentle, comfortable, not too tight. The camera remains on his hands as he goes through his routine of three practice putts … minimal movement, all parts of the grip locked together into a unit, restrained. The camera angle shifts now to show him standing over the putt; I am focusing only on his head. Woods taps his putt firmly, and his head remains still for a *full* second. The ball drops into the center of the cup. Try to picture this whole process in your mind's eye. If you have not seen Tiger Woods do this, try to use the above description to visualize it.

One more lesson: Woods tries for a twenty-footer on 18 for birdie. Again, I watch his head, and though the putt misses the hole by about four inches and rolls six feet past the hole, I count a full second between when his putter makes contact with the ball and when I see the bill of his cap turn toward the pin. I predict he will sink the par putt coming back ... yep, dead center of the cup. He sinks the six-footer, and the "bill of the cap" effect is again *very* evident. Check it for yourself. Watch him for a few rounds in any tournament he plays. He's not just a legend in his own time; he's a walking golf lesson. I'm sure that whenever you're reading this, Woods will still be playing, and he won't have changed this one simple component of his golfing profile—not one bit.

One additional image from Bay Hill: At the same tournament, one day shy of exactly a year later, host Arnold Palmer stood motionless at the edge of the 18th green surrounded by hundreds of fans in the gallery. They were all, to a person, transfixed as Tiger Woods, at nine under par for the tournament, carefully measured the twenty-four foot birdie putt he needed to steal the tournament championship from Bart Bryant who was already in the clubhouse himself at nine-under and expecting, or perhaps the more appropriate word would be "hoping," to compete against Woods in a playoff. With the drone of an airplane overhead, a fish crow croaking from the nearby woods, and a lone double-crested cormorant feeding in the pond below the green, Woods went through his routine, taking long minutes studying the green's slopes, texture, grain, distances—and we can only vaguely imagine what else. He finally stood over his putt, followed the routine described above, and calmly sent the ball at just the right speed slowly down the gentle slope toward the water until it curled to the right at the last minute and dropped gently into the cup—vintage Tiger Woods. If the film is still available on the web, you can see for yourself at:

http://ballhype.com/video/tiger_woods_bay_hill_2008_18th_hole_1/

Watch the three-minute film all the way through because there is a stirring moment between Woods and Arnold Palmer at the end.

Here's another way for you to see whether I'm right or not. Putt in your living room or out on the practice green. Read the putt, get your line and your distance, do your practice putts, then step up to your ball, get the putter in place—and close your eyes. Then putt and leave your eyes closed. I maintain that your putting will be no worse with your eyes closed, and might eventually even get better. This is not my own drill. You might already have read it in another book and started practicing it.

Just do what you need to do to test the theory that holding your head still for a full second *after* contact insures that your line will be true. Later, you can cut it down to a split second after you've confirmed for yourself that I am right. Now remember this: it might not be the *right* line, but whatever line it is, it will not morph into a different line due to head movement. The same thing is true on drives and fairway shots, shots out of the rough, lob wedge shots, and so on. That split second, for all of its brevity and innocuousness, has a huge impact on your game.

A quick sidebar here: I've lost track of the number of times I've said to myself, "Do it right the first time, Dummy!" Home construction projects, research papers for graduate school, throwing the frisbee for my dog, getting directions and then arriving at a destination on time, saying something important to someone important—*and* golf shots. Doing things right the first time just means being mindful enough (see Chapter 2) to make the necessary preparations ahead of time in order to increase the chances that the action *will*, in fact, be right.

Another aphorism that's getting quite a bit of play these days is this one: "There are no re-dos in life." If that is the case, and there is an ever expanding amount of evidence to suggest that it is, then doing things right the first time should be a top shelf objective for all of us, bogey golfers and the rest.

I'm suggesting that it is well worth it to take the importance of this split-second theory seriously for a while, at least to see if it makes a difference for you. It may not be on the countless Top Ten Techniques lists you'll find in books on the golf shelf at bookstores, but if you haven't yet figured out that I'm trying to focus on a few of the little things related to golfing technique, you're missing my point. I'm not concerned with big-ticket tips. You can get those from any lesson, any video, any magazine, any golf pro, or maybe even your playing partner. Try to do what is necessary to avoid having to say to yourself, "Do it right the first time, Dummy!" after your shots. That will be a very important achievement. Mis-hits, bad reads, or poor lines do not necessarily mean that you didn't do it right the first time, but only you can know for sure whether or not you took enough time to prepare for the shot. And only you will know if you have made the best use of the most important split second in golf.

CHAPTER ELEVEN
PUTTING: THE WAY OF THE GREEN

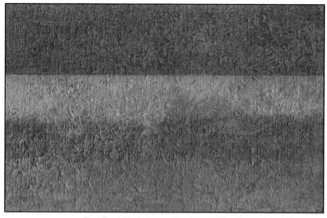

Red Rock Variations – The Way of the Green: Hard Distance
by George Morrison from the collection of Thomas Osborn.

It looked good a long way, and I
thought, this has got a chance. And then
three feet out, I thought, oh, this is going
in, and then it started diving across
the front of the hole a little bit, and I
thought, it might not.

Adam Scott, *on
sinking a dramatic forty-nine-foot putt to
win the 2008 Byron Nelson Championship
on the third hole of a sudden-death playoff*

These greens are so fast I have to hold
my putter over the ball and hit it with
the shadow.

Sam Snead

Not all that many years ago, and some years before I began playing golf, I had a small acrylic painting by Minnesota artist George Morrison hanging in my living room. Morrison was a Chippewa Indian who grew up on the North Shore of Lake Superior and received his art education in Minneapolis, New York, and Paris. He passed away in 2000, but he left us an impressive body of work and a persistent memory of his way as an artist. Several of his works can be seen in Minneapolis almost without getting out of your car: the twenty-one-foot tall totem in LaSalle Plaza, the exterior wall of the American Indian Center, and the granite mosaic on Nicollet Mall to name three. In 2005, and along with Southwestern sculptor Alan Houser, Morrison was honored with a special exhibit at the newly opened National Museum of the American Indian in Washington, D.C. His work is rich in its composition, yet full of quiet distinctiveness. He imbues each of his works with an abiding sense of how the pieces of one's life fit together like a puzzle, and a humble and pervasive awareness of The Creator's influence in the world. In a career that spanned more than fifty years, Morrison created both two-dimensional and three-dimensional works using a wide variety of media. Every so often, during a lazy round of golf on a quiet summer day with Superior's sapphire-colored expanse within a slight turn of my head, I'll imagine it as a vast Morrison painting out there, dappled, colorful, and serene.

The painting I owned was one of his so-called Red Rock Variations, a series sometimes referred to as the Horizon paintings. He painted these small abstract works late in his career. They're done in acrylic and framed in metal and driftwood, the elegant pastel colors suggesting the many moods of Lake Superior. The one that graced my living room for a few years contains a narrow "fairway" of forest green running through a blue and amber mix, with Morrison's signature horizon line a third of the way down from the top.

Putting: The Way of the Green

I think of that painting often. I miss its steadying and organic wholeness. I sold the painting before I took up golf, but in some ineffable way, my memory of its green tranquility influences how I play and how I feel when I play. When I am walking on golf greens, I try to recapture the deep relaxation I used to feel looking at that painting. It is fitting, and hardly coincidental, that the title of that painting happens to be "The Way of the Green: Hard Distance."

More than any aspect of this game, putting can affect how you feel about yourself, about life, about your next appointment, about the day, about the balance of nature, and even about things that words are simply not adequate to describe. I am not being purposely enigmatic here. Putting requires a mental relaxation, a delicacy of movement, and a spiritual tranquility rarely required elsewhere. I liken it to coaxing a fussy baby back to sleep, rebuilding an engine, tying a dry fly, embroidery, glass blowing, perhaps training a dog. You need to be in the right frame of mind before you tackle the job; you need to have patience enough to contend with mistakes of your own or with the "way of the green"—or for that matter, the way of the ball. If you're going to play bogey golf, there are some hard distances you will have to travel on the putting green that cannot be traveled if either your road map or your compass is in bad repair.

So much for metaphors. In Chapter 3, there is a section on putting that you have hopefully committed to memory. I want to add a few things here that will help you to travel the hard distance successfully, and though you may never become a great putter, you certainly should expect to become a *good* putter after paying attention to some of these suggestions, that is, if you are not *already* a good putter. I do realize that many, and very likely a majority of you are better golfers than I am. But our own formulas, routines, habits, and peculiar ways of approaching challenges might be worth sharing with one another no matter how well we play. For those of us who will never compete professionally, there is much to be said for and much to be gained from sharing the wealth, pooling our talents, and settling into an easy give and take with one another, free from the edgy and even miserly way in which some competitors at the professional level have to play the game. I want to add, though, that no sport offers as many opportunities for doing this kind of pooling resources. Books, lessons, video and audio tapes, live action or Internet film clips, conversations and interviews, informal conversations at the range or on the practice green, or just talking amiably during play are all very easy ways to freshen up how we approach putting. Golf's accessibility is one of its most delightful and wholesome facets.

When I putt on my living room rug, I pay attention to just three things:

Putting Tip 1:

The first thing is to determine whether or not the takeaway is smooth and comfortable. That is often where the first sign of trouble can show up. I frequently see (*and* feel) the putter wiggle as I take it back to begin the putt. Actually, it's less the putter than my upper arms; the movement of the putter is actually the after effect. I haven't figured out why that happens, but I work on that part of putting quite a bit. One thing that influences the takeaway for me is whether or not the putter is touching the ground. If the putter is touching the ground, I not only have to take it back, but I have to lift it up slightly as well. This little wrinkle seems to make for a slight jerky wiggle that can be very distracting when I'm trying to follow a line, develop pace, and strike the ball with just the right amount of acceleration. I know that some golfers would argue that resting the putter on the ground ever so slightly settles it and allows your arms to be at rest. It is simply a matter of how it feels, so figure out what works best for you.

Putting Tip 2:

I pay attention to whether or not my arms, wrists, hands, and fingers feel like an integrated unit. This is actually the logical next step once I have experienced the wiggle just mentioned. Locking everything up from my shoulders down through the tip of my fingers allows the putter to follow a straight line from beginning to end. It may not necessarily be the *right* line, but that is a separate problem. Experiencing the feel of having the mechanism or the machinery of that unit locked from your shoulders to your grip is a sure-fire way to make the putt *feel* more like a real putt. Couple that with your line work—or call it your target line work—*and* the tips from Chapter 3, and you should have enough to work on in your living room until you can get out on a real putting green.

135

Putting Tip 3:

The final thing I think about is follow-through. But first, I want to mention again the importance of follow-through in general. I won't get up on a soapbox—and I have to confess to not being a particularly good role model myself—but at least as far as golf is concerned, if you are a good follow-through person, that's a whole back pack full of troubles you will not have to deal with. There may be a little tweaking here and there that might be helpful, even necessary, but there can be no denying the positive results that come from having confident follow-through, and that is true whether you're on the golf course or not. As for putting, the advice is simple: follow-through on your putts and finish pointing at the target. It's a simple thing to practice on your living room rug. I keep referring to that specific practice technique because, as I have mentioned, where I live there are no golf greens available from November through the middle of April. (As a matter of fact, as I edit this chapter right now, it is April 26, 2008, and it has been snowing off and on all day.) Now, even at golf domes or practice ranges, the putting greens are usually flat as pancakes, just like the living room rug. So what about breaks and slopes? Somehow, you have to figure out how to practice reading breaks, which may require considerable ingenuity with your living room rug, or heading south in the winter. You need real slopes on putting surfaces to learn the heady art of reading the way putts will break on a slope.

I devised a little goal-setting formula for putting. If we can come close to reaching this goal, bogey golf is easily within striking distance. The formula starts with a cold hard fact: the pros at the top of the statistical chart for average putts fall somewhere between 1.7 and 1.8 putts per hole. That means the average number of putts per hole is more than one and a half, or fewer than two. And this stands to reason, for no one is going to one-putt every hole, but they all know how to avoid three-putting, and most of the world's best golfers putt well enough to keep their average just below two putts per hole. So, where does that leave us would-be bogey golfers? Here's my formula and how I arrive at it:

1. Bogey golf means shooting a 90 for eighteen holes.

2. That's an extra stroke a hole, or seventy-two strokes (par) plus eighteen strokes (bogey).

3. If you three-putt a hole, chances are you may be using up *at least* two more strokes than bogey golf allows you to use, *unless* you can reach the green in regulation consistently. "On the green in regulation" means reaching the green with just one stroke on par 3s, two strokes on par 4s, and three strokes on par 5s; par always allows you two strokes once you are on the green.

4. But most of us, if given an extra stroke on each hole, are most likely going to need that stroke out on the fairway, the adjacent woods, a bunker, or the like.

5. That means that you have to do whatever it takes to avoid three-putting so you can "bank" that extra stroke for your use out on the fairway.

6. Two-putting is what you should focus on—in your mind as well as in your living room, on the practice green, in the golf dome, at the putting sections in the golf shops, because …

7. … if you average exactly three putts per hole … well, do the math: that's more than half of the total number of shots allowable for eighteen holes of bogey golf.

No matter how you look at it, putting is the easiest part of the game to practice. It is also the very best way to keep your scores hovering in the vicinity of bogey—once you have most of your swing skills and your distance calculation skills and your club selection skills at a comfortable level.

Here's a little game to help improve your putting, one that you can play on your own or not, it doesn't really matter. If you're playing with someone else, however, make sure your partner is comfortable with you doing this, and you *shouldn't* do it on busy days at the course because it will take extra time:

The Putting Game:

From your approach shot to sinking the final putt, play two balls. See if you can *always* get at least a little closer on each of your *second* shots. *But*—when it comes to recording your score, you *must go with the score you earn using the farthest ball away from the cup <u>after</u> you putt both balls once.* You must get your first approach shot and your first putt as close to the hole as possible. You can, of course, do this on the practice green instead. This can easily replace doing it on the course, thereby saving your party or the party behind you from having to wait for you.

It is easier to invent putting games than for any other aspect of golf. When my IPP and I finish a round, and especially if the scores are close and there is no one immediately behind us, we will often invent games on the putting surface of the final hole. We get to prolong the round, raise the stakes, stay out in the sun longer, give the loser a chance to win it all back, or just plain practice. The way we typically do it is to play something like this:

Game 1:

Players putt three (or two) balls from the same random spot more than ten feet away from the pin and keep putting until they're all in; lowest stroke total for all balls wins.

Game 2:

Players take turns putting consecutive balls from a starting point until each

player fails to get a putt closer than his
preceding putt; then players putt their
closest balls into the hole; fewest total
strokes wins.

Game 3:

Start with three (or two) balls apiece;
take turns; first one to sink all three (or
two) of them wins.

In February of 2008, I visited my club pro, Paul Schintz, to see
about getting this book into the pro shop after publication.
Schintz is the type of pro who hits balls whenever and
wherever he gets the opportunity including in the middle of
a Northern Minnesota winter. He is well-known for hitting
range balls off the roof of the clubhouse throughout winter
until either the snow melts or he runs out of balls.

On this particular visit, I drove into the snow covered parking
lot to find him right outside the downstairs doorway hitting
three woods off a piece of carpeting. It was twenty-three
degrees outside, and he was hitting three woods like it was the
middle of July. An hour later, after our chat inside, he grabbed
his putter from the back room, and before I knew it, I was in
the middle of a putting lesson on the floor of the clubhouse.
He taught me something as critical to successful putting as
the tip in Chapter 10 about head movement. He reminded me
about line and speed, the two requirements for a putt. Schintz
uses the water pipe against the wall right next to his office as
the flagstick, and sets the ball down about fifteen or twenty
feet away. He talked about lining up the putt before you
address the ball. While he was doing this, he noticed that I was
eyeing the ungainly tilt in the very old floor quite close to the

pipe. "I have to line my ball up with that little break in mind, too," he said with a wry smile.

I watched as he squatted low to the floor and carefully matched the line on his ball with the path he wanted the ball to travel. He adjusted the line slightly to the right of the pipe, and then stood up, explaining that this procedure gets one of the two requirements of a good putt out of the way when you stand over your putt. All he had to think about now was speed because line had already been taken care of. He took two practice putts, and then addressed the ball being careful to align the manufacturer's mark on his putter with the line on the ball. He moved the putter back slowly, then back down sending the ball on its way. The ball rolled on a line well to the right of the pipe, and then about three feet away from the wall it began to curl toward the pipe. A second later, there was a dull metallic clank as the ball hit the pipe squarely in the middle.

I tried a putt, and though the ball started out on the same line, I hit it too hard and its curl was noticeably less pronounced. It slammed into the molding some eight inches to the right of the pipe. Schintz putted again from a different location with nearly the same result. I have the image of him practicing to his heart's content with an entire putting green set up in the midst of chairs, tables, and boxes of golf shoes. I'm doubtful about creating even one "hole" for practice in my living room, but I am nevertheless grateful to have added another bit of wisdom to this chapter thanks to Schintz. Though putting seems to be a simple act, I have once again learned that the words simple and complicated often nest quite comfortably together when it comes to golf. Lao Tsu says as much in the *Tao Te Ching*.

See simplicity in the complicated.

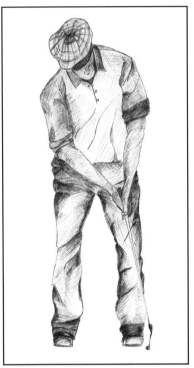

"Peeking" too soon can alter your line.   Keep eyes on spot where the ball was.

As I mention in the first paragraph, the words "hard distance" are part of the title of George Morrison's painting, and though the gap between the ball and the flagstick often does seem to be a hard distance, the real challenge is to contend with and ultimately master the hard distance within ourselves, the one between a comfortable and confident self on the one hand, and an anxious, tightly wrapped, fearful self on the other.

When I watch the pros in televised matches, it always amazes me how well most of them keep a poker face even when their putts are not falling. On the putting green, they are like tightrope walkers. To reach the two-putt goal, you, too, have to shut distractions out, even while you are gauging such things as how hard or softly to strike the putt, where the break will be, what your line is, whether there is a slope, what the grain of the grass is, how long or short it has been cut ... and other things, too, like wind, temperature, moisture ... the list can be discouraging even before you realize how important it also is to relax, not think too much, and commit to the shot. The more comfortable and relaxed you can be as you plan your putt, the more your own hard distance will continually shorten.

"The Way of the Green" has its own integrity, but recognizing this is secondary to recognizing how important it is for you to find "The Way of Your Self." If you can make that discovery, you will actually begin looking forward to putting. Even though it can drive you crazy, even though there will be days when you say (as my IPP and I occasionally say to one another mostly joking) "I might quit this game," even though putts will fall for you one day and rim out, lip out, stop short, run past, or miss by a hair the next—despite *all* of this, you want to establish a "Way" for yourself, one that withstands these unpredictable and random turns. The more you practice putting, the faster that "Way" will come for you on golf greens.

Make your putter your friend, cherish it, treat it with respect and dignity, and you will be amazed at how soon it will begin to respond, perform, and shine. It will start to make the possibility of bogey golf a little brighter than just a small light at the end of a very long tunnel.

Chapter Twelve
Jekyll and Hyde Golf

> ... bounding from my bed, I rushed to the mirror. At the sight that met my eyes, my blood was changed into something exquisitely thin and icy. Yes, I had gone to bed Henry Jekyll, I had awakened Edward Hyde.
>
> Robert Louis Stevenson

> In golf, as in no other sport, your principal opponent is yourself.
>
> Herbert Warren Wind

I've been playing golf seriously for eight seasons—that's all. But I have already found it to be an invaluable substitute for my therapist's couch. Let's see ... one hundred dollars an hour as a couch potato and guaranteed deep discouragement from time to time, versus about five dollars an hour using my season pass and guaranteed deep discouragement from time to time—ah, but *plus* nature, conversation, humor, gamesmanship, and a hot dog and a beer afterward ... along with insights into my game, my self, and my life, and at the same time get some good exercise. That's a pretty rare bargain.

The only problem is that sometimes the insights can seriously jeopardize the exercise, as on the day when I realized with all the shock of the first quote above that I was playing Jekyll and Hyde golf. If you don't know who Dr. Jekyll and Mr. Hyde are, read *Dr. Jekyll and Mr. Hyde*. It is a short book, but horrifyingly relevant for those of us who struggle mightily with more than one personality when we bravely set out to do our best in a game that can, in a heartbeat, turn you from mellow to monstrous.

My IPP likes to tell the story of the day when he watched in horror as I morphed from a golfing buddy into a drooling ghoul, bellowing loud oafish curses at the top of my lungs—*after a practice swing!* It's true, and I remember it even better than he does because it was the first time I experienced what this chapter is all about. I was taking my routine practice swings in the usual nonchalant manner when one of them dug into the turf, sending numbing shock waves deep into my somewhat arthritic wrists. What followed remains to this day a legend between me and my IPP … and the occasion of fits of laughter among our friends whenever golfing stories are exchanged in polite company.

The swing is the best indicator of your psychic stability on the golf course—and maybe elsewhere as well. Don't pay any attention at all to whether or not the ball lands neatly in the fairway or drops quickly into the cup on the green. It's not about whether your score is anywhere near your career best, or whether the ball does what you want it to do every time you swing the club. *It's all about the swing.* I remember one four iron shot, on a downhill lie, that I deftly bent around a promontory of trees and over a little knoll. It landed out of sight, yet I knew instinctively that the lie would be beautiful. That shot felt like a million bucks, and indeed, when I approached the ball, I started fantasizing about the shot of a lifetime, and how memorable this hole would be—all because of the humble four iron—and then on the next stroke, a simple chip shot from inside fifty yards, the bottom edge of my pitching wedge hit the ball square in the middle. The ball instantly became what baseball players refer to as a "frozen rope," a sizzling line drive less than three feet off the ground that hit once just in front of the green and ricocheted all the way across and into the brush ten yards or so behind the green. I had felt like the King of the Course after the four iron shot, but after that bestial wedge shot, I felt like a misbegotten demon. Seriously!

The best thing—the only thing—that you can do about Jekyll and Hyde golf is to come to terms with the simple fact that it happens. If it happens to the pros on occasion, you can be sure it's going to happen to you. And it can strike you when you least expect it to. You hit a good shot, and you say to yourself, "Finally! I thought a shot like that would *never* happen!" And the next thing, it happens. It begins in a place none of us ever spend much time thinking about, a place that has no name. It's just there somewhere inside, and something shuts off—or turns on—in there. You think you own the course, you think your problems are solved, you think your troubles are over because you finally did something **right** on the golf course, and you think now that, at long last, you can relax. The truth of the matter is

No, you can't.

Precisely the time *not* to relax is after a good shot, and this is doubly true after a great shot. Make that after a **bad** shot as well. Maybe you're catching on here: ebbs and flows in your mental state are not good. Neither are peaks and valleys, or highs and lows, or ups and downs. These all can morph ever so quickly and insidiously into Jekyll and Hyde golf, and why? **Because you let your guard down**. You come unglued. You think you own the place. You want to quit this game. You hate yourself. You love yourself. You hate golf. You love golf. You want to make love with your clubs. You want to throw them into the duck pond. You're ready for the tour. You're going to march right down to Play It Again, Sports and give them back your clubs … *free … **through the window!*** You're thinking seriously of flying to Florida for lessons and a week of golf in the sun with free drinks and food at night, and you're going to lower your handicap by ten strokes because you finally have found The Truth about how golf and life are so interdependent and you don't know how you could ever go back to your old ways on the golf course, not to mention life as you knew it before this moment … take a look around you when you're feeling like this. Listen to the wind in the lofty Norway pines over at the side of the fairway or the bluebirds chirruping softly and delicately in the emerald green quaking aspen saplings in between fairways. Jekyll and Hyde golf is giving in to extremes, and at our level, where we aspire to play bogey golf in spite of struggling just to break 100, extremes of this kind will sink us ninety-nine times out of one hundred.

This is not at all about *embracing* Jekyll and Hyde golf and thereby defeating it. This chapter is about understanding that such experiences are pretty much the way of it unless and until you can see your way through these two extremes to a path of more or less consistent physical control. I have to add one more proviso here, so that you don't get the wrong idea and start faking it. You can't pretend to be cool or mellow or in a Zen state about everything on the outside if you're a writhing Medusa on the inside.

That was the problem with Dr. Henry Jekyll. His exterior was simply a mask for the interior Mr. Edward Hyde. Somehow or other, we have to devise a plan for putting Mr. Hyde to sleep with a very powerful and long-lasting sedative in order to let the respectable, the gentle, the purposeful Dr. Jekyll do his thing. In other words, we have to develop control and serenity that are real, reliable, and routine. It's a tall order but it's not impossible—even for the most explosive, hypercritical, judgmental, or obsessive of personalities.

CHAPTER TWELVE

I have to state here, parenthetically but nonetheless emphatically, that I am not talking about becoming a Zen Master. *That* particular state of mind might be too distanced from the realities of the game and require too much in the way of training at the feet of some guru or other. I remember trying once to adopt the "Zen Master" approach. It prompted a fairly cynical response from my IPP and also from his teen-aged daughter who happened to be playing with us that day. I announced in no uncertain terms, shouting it across the fairway after a particularly miserable series of shots, that "from here on out, you're going to be playing with the Zen Master!" A deep silence followed. The two of them exchanged glances. We played on, and the silence grew louder. The pressure was beginning to build, stroke by stroke. I felt like I was in a library, or worse, a church … a Zen center of my own creation.

It wasn't long before a very tortured soul uttered an unearthly bellow, having just sculled a brand-new Top Flight deep into the woods with a foul smelling six iron hook from right in the middle of the fairway. I had transformed myself from Zen Master to Mr. Hyde openly. After a long silence, I heard the quiet voice of my IPP's daughter ask softly from across the fairway, "What happened to the Zen Master?"

"_____ *the Zen Master!!!!*"

was all I could yell, and my plan for instant transformation lay in ruins. From that day to this, the Zen Master Story runs a close second to the Practice Swing Story. I note here, with grim humility, that the two funniest stories about my playing habits appear here—in the chapter about Jekyll and Hyde golf.

But now, I am a new man. I don't aspire to be a Zen Master anymore, and I am working on sending Mr. Hyde to bed—for good. I don't think I can ever kill him, but dormancy is a distinct possibility, and the effect is just as good. Here's my Ten-Step Recipe for how to do it:

1. Think of golf as play, not as work.

2. Create modest, short-term, baby step-goals for yourself.

3. Build in fun stuff both on the course and in practice.

4. See the beauty around you, and find a connection between it and your game.

5. Listen to the birds.

6. Have a few favorite holes even if you don't always play them well.

7. Find an IPP, and learn how to talk with yourself when your IPP can't play.

8. Take delight in the flight of the ball.

9. Pay attention to happy accidents.

10. Consider the possibility that some of them are not accidents.

Some of the items on this list are self explanatory, I trust. Simple ones like "Listen to the birds" are all about paying attention to, and in some way or another giving thanks for things that make the game so unique and so rejuvenating. If you listen closely enough, it's not going to be too long before you can actually tell a blue bird from a blue jay or a downy woodpecker from a pileated woodpecker or a crow from a raven. [Note: Currently, tentative efforts are being made to lure Ben Crenshaw into the broadcast booth from time to time to do short spots about the local birds that can be heard or seen in the background at some televised PGA events. Crenshaw, who won the 1984 and the 1995 Masters Tournaments, is said to be a birdwatcher.]

As I mention in an earlier chapter, I feel very fortunate to have my home course so situated above Lake Superior that on several holes, the western end of the lake is in full view. In fact, such views rather upstage the game. It's not uncommon for my IPP, who grew up in Duluth, to remark at the passing of a thousand-footer approaching the Duluth harbor to pick up taconite from the Iron Range or grain from western Minnesota. Paying attention to our surroundings does two things for our golf game. First, it removes some of the intense focus on results and allows us to focus a bit more on the process. Second, it allows us to feel more a part of the landscape, a little closer to it and less detached from it, which, in turn, makes for a much less self-centered attitude about the play. There can be little doubt that a large part of Jekyll and Hyde golf originates in being too self-centered, even narcissistic about such things as what our score is, how long our drives are, whether we're putting better than our playing partners, and so on.

And speaking of playing partners, playing with someone you know fairly well and with whom you can share idle as well as serious conversation makes all the difference in the world. My brother is lucky enough to be married to a wonderful woman with whom he plays golf on a regular basis. They are very evenly matched and often play with another couple with whom they also socialize. I've played many times in their group, and it is delightful. There can hardly be a better arrangement when it comes to finding common ground among friends and within a marriage. When sedated by the happy camaraderie of friends and family in a round of golf, Mr. Hyde tends toward a bit more torpor.

A word about happy accidents. Last spring while walking my dog, I found a golf ball, a perfect Titleist 4, deep in the woods near my home. Golf was the furthest thing from my mind that day, but suddenly I'm looking at the gleaming white perfection of a clean, new golf ball nestled among the twigs and leaves on the bank of a meandering woodland creek several miles from the nearest golf course. A Titleist at that! I didn't really attach much significance to the find; I assumed someone had been hitting golf balls into the woods from the field across the street and didn't care to retrieve them.

A few weeks later, I took the ball with me to a member-guest tournament I played in with my brother in New York. I started the first round with the woodland ball, intending to carry some of its "magic" into this more serious and competitive event. We were playing brilliantly most of the morning, and for three holes I felt particularly empowered by my Minnesota talisman. Then, about halfway through our round, it happened. After a fluid nine iron approach shot that felt virtually perfect, I had watched with exhilaration as the ball arched up into the canopied area near the green (see 8 above) when the ball disappeared.

It turned out that it fell into a pond I had forgotten about since the last time I had played the course. I was heartsick for a moment, but I knew I couldn't allow this insignificant event to derail what had started out as a fine round of golf. Instead, I tried to think about the fact that I was leaving some Minnesota magic in a New York golf course pond, and maybe it would be a rare find for another golfer as it had been for me—so I reached in my golf bag and pulled out another ball. After all, I told myself, "seen one ball, an' you've seen 'em all."

Every golfer has a bagful of stories about lucky bounces. I remember several such bounces in the short time I've been playing, but I felt that a few of them were somehow designed to do more than just keep my ball in play. There's always that lucky bounce that rescues a bad hole or a bad round, but every so often you experience some quirky unexpected twist that rescues you from the grasp of an awakened Mr. Hyde and you wind up smiling to yourself. To benefit from such miracles, you may have to reconcile yourself to one of the magnificent paradoxes in golf: sometimes a bad shot turns into a good one despite our best efforts.

Once in a while, something deeper happens that reaffirms the presence of forces out there that can defy, perhaps even counteract our fallibility. In other words, you can hit a bad shot and discover that, with apologies to Robert Frost, "something there is that doesn't love a bad shot." A force exists within the game that works to preserve itself even when we are doing our level best to ignore, resist, or disprove it. For some, it's more comfortable to stick with the "luck" explanation, but the two do not preclude one another. In their own way, they both make it clear to us that golf has a special quality that sometimes, not always, but sometimes, works in our favor even when we stink. We have to remain open or receptive to that possibility for it to add a whole different dimension to our game. So, think about 10 above ... at least *consider* the possibility. Think of it as an easy antidote to Hyde's unpredictable wakefulness.

Finally, I want to say a few things about partners because it's a significant aspect of the game at our level. I can honestly say that during the eight summers in which I have played serious golf, I have had no fewer than a dozen moments when I felt so connected to the person or persons I was playing with that I lost track of everything else that was not directly related to that person or those people. Statistics and scores, time of day, eventual outcome, handicap, birdie, bogey, par—all of that vanished into thin air when my brothers and I finished with identical scores once a few summers ago; when my colleague screamed and yelled at the top of her lungs and jumped up and down after she saw me sink a bump-and-run with a nine iron from ten feet off the green; when my IPP broke 40 for nine holes on his birthday; when my brother and I shot a birdie on a long par 5 in a best-ball round; when my IPP and his daughter both sank seven iron chips from off the green on the same hole; when a complete stranger played along with me and out of the clear blue sky gave me the idea for this book; when I broke 50 for the first time on a sunny summer morning playing alone; when my brother and I were still in the hunt at the member-guest after the first day of our first try at it; and all the times when my IPP and I would delay teeing off on 7 of the Lakes Nine as long as we could, just to look out at Lake Superior.

Hyde will sleep long and peacefully when you are open to deep encounters with cosmic rhythms and the power of friendship outdoors. Getting to bogey golf is best advanced, ironic as it may seem, by focusing less on the product you desire and more on the process you use in seeking it.

CHAPTER THIRTEEN
INTENTION AND EXECUTION

Some people try to find things
in this game that don't exist,
but football is only two things -
blocking and tackling.

Vince Lombardi

What other people may find in poetry
or art museums, I find in the flight of a
good drive.

Arnold Palmer

I remember Vince Lombardi's arrival in Green Bay like it was yesterday. We grew up in St. Paul, but my brothers and I had gotten used to watching the Green Bay Packers lose nearly every game in the 1957 and 1958 NFL seasons on our family's first television set, a black-and-white 23" Sylvania. In 1959, Lombardi's first year as head coach, the Packers won seven games and lost five, and the next year won eight games and lost four. In just his second year as head coach, Lombardi had the Packers playing the Philadelphia Eagles for the NFL Championship. It was to be Lombardi's only loss in a championship game. If it had not been for Eagles linebacker Chuck Bednarik, who played fifty-eight of the sixty minutes of that game, the Green Bay coach may well have owned a perfect championship record.

It was the final play of the game. With thirteen seconds left in the game, Green Bay trailed the Eagles by a score of 17–13, but the Packers were at the Philadelphia twenty-two yard line. Bart Starr, now in the NFL Hall of Fame, hit a short pass to fellow Hall-of-Famer Jim Taylor, who made it down to the eight yard line before being unceremoniously tackled in the open field by Bednarik, the last Eagle between Taylor and the goal line. Here's how the thirty-five-year old Bednarik remembered the tackle that gave the Eagles their third league championship:

> I guess everyone was covered downfield, because he threw a little swing pass to Taylor, who caught it and then put his head down and started running. The clock was ticking. A couple of our guys tried to tackle him, but he was a big guy, and they just bounced off him. He must have run about fifteen or sixteen yards already when he came rumbling toward me. I was the only one standing between him and the end zone, so I knew I had to tackle him. I gave him a big bear-hug tackle up high and wrestled him to the ground at the nine-yard line. Laying there on top of him, I could see the game clock ticking down: five ... four ... three ... two ... one ... zero.

Bednarik's tackle is one of the NFL's most historic ones. Lombardi's dedication to perfecting the fundamentals—to the importance of the "only two things, blocking and tackling"—made it a cruel irony as well.

Some golfers like to say that golf is only two things, too: tempo and timing, or driving and putting, or focus and rhythm. My nomination for the most basic two things in golf is equally elemental, but I like it better because it is mental and physical, commitment paired with actual performance. My "blocking and tackling" is this: *intention* and *execution*.

Like other aspects of this book, this observation will probably elicit a "Duh!" or "Is *that* right?" or "You think?" reaction. Bogey golf is out of the question, however, unless and until you make this pair of words an integral part of your consciousness every time you're on a golf course: intention and execution. Know what your intention is and then execute it to the best of your ability using a practiced mindfulness. For most of us who aspire to play bogey golf, this "practiced mindfulness" means that we have to assume good shots will rarely happen as a matter of course. Therefore, on each shot, we have to compensate, and that happens by first focusing on or visualizing what our intention is until it's firmly in mind. Then we have to make that visualization happen—to execute.

I seriously doubt that there is a sport or a game to which this rule does not apply. If it is so obvious and prevalent, then why spend a whole chapter on it? What else is there to say? Even if we come to this idea from complete innocence or ignorance, how much more can we add to the phrase "intention and execution" to make it more accessible and more useful? Maybe it's just this: if you get it, then go and do it.

I maintain that however easy it is to say, and however pat or stock it sounds, keeping an "intention and execution" mindset going for one hole, let alone nine or eighteen holes, is no small accomplishment. I am beginning to understand what separates the touring pros from all other players, which is that their mental approach to the game is resilient, dependable, and sinewy. It has no body fat on it whatsoever. It is difficult, of course; only the best career players know how to develop, tweak, plan, and execute an intention consistently over the course of several years. It's hard enough to do *once* during a round; imagine what it means to a player for whom this habit kicks in automatically on every hole of every round, match or practice, year after year.

These two words are certainly distinct from one another in many ways, but even though we're talking about a two-word phrase, they are not entirely separate components of a particular stroke. There must be elements of the intention within the execution, and vice versa. I will stop short of getting technical at this point. I'll skip the percentages and fractions and point break-downs because I have no idea what they are. What I do know is that when you are looking 150 yards down the fairway at the flagstick—with its little blue, white, red, striped, or logo-embossed flag waving gently in the breeze, teasing you to try to go for it all—you are definitely thinking, even if it might be subconsciously, about both the intention and the execution while focusing consciously only on your intention.

So for the moment, let's assume that without a good intention, there is very little chance of having any sort of decent execution. The time, energy, and decision-making skill that formulating a good intention requires will most of the time have a nice payoff even if the shot is a little short, or a little wide, or a little strong. The concentration required to develop an intention is not, I repeat *not*, a matter of intense contemplation. It shouldn't take more than a couple of minutes. In fact, I can remember certain holes where I'd start thinking about my *intention* right after the previous shot, so that when I arrived at the ball, I felt like I had already done most of the hard work.

Work? It's always slightly amusing to think of anything in this game as "work," by the way. Can you imagine? *Work*? It's *play*, for heaven's sakes: *P—L—A—Y*. For the professionals, it is work because it is their livelihood, but we are not pros. Relaxation and remembering to think of golf as play, especially when we aspire to shoot bogey golf, is good for your game and for your mind. Remember this point, for it tends to diminish the pressure you put on yourself.

Formulating an intention involves commitment (see Chapter 5) from which springs another trio of commitments essential to your intention. This list is the idea of licensed sports psychologist Deborah Graham, whose organization, GolfPsych is at www.golfpsych.com. I found it in a book called *Be the Ball* (see Chapter 6). Dr. Graham's philosophy is surely a mantra for just about every golfer who has learned to do "intention and execution" as a matter of course. Graham instructs her students to "commit to three things: the club, the target, and the type of shot."

Again:

> *1. commit to the club*
> *2. commit to the target*
> *3. commit to the type of shot*

Easy enough, right? I can do the first one quite quickly. It's not a matter of specific yardage as it is for the pros and the scratch golfers. I'm at the "close enough" stage. I can satisfy myself with saying fairly quickly,

> "I'm about 125 yards out with a only gentle uphill slope, so this is an eight iron shot. Period. End of discussion."

I'm sure that somehow, sometimes, my IPP will read my mind from all the way across the fairway and say something like,

"I hope you're not thinking about using your eight iron." I wonder if he hasn't known in some uncanny way that I was working on this book and perhaps on this very chapter at the moment he says that. "He's testing my commitment," I think to myself. In our early summers, I'd immediately start second-guessing myself after his not-so-innocent inquiry, and I'd start thinking that maybe a nine iron would be a better choice. More often than not, indecision like this winds up having disastrous results, and the reason is simple: an absence of commitment.

I'm certain that you can find examples from your own golf game, and other areas of your life as well, where indecision led to unsatisfactory results. Using this simple example as a guide, you can actually discover the real benefit of commitment outside your golf game if you can become mindful about it inside your golf game. But back to my IPP.

It's not that I distrust what he says right away at such a moment. Hardly. My IPP has been playing golf much longer than I have, so I tend to listen quite carefully when he offers an opinion, especially if I have asked for it. We joke occasionally about his being my caddie, about his knowing my game better than he knows his own. So I don't really distrust what he says when it comes to choosing a club. What I have now developed, rather, is more confidence in knowing my own abilities and my own decision-making skills. My IPP gives me a robust "you were right, and I was wrong" affirmation if my club choice turns out to be correct. What a pleasure!

If committing to a club is the easiest of the three, then committing to the target is the second-easiest one. This point might seem like another "Duh!" situation, but hold on. The target isn't always completely visible. It depends first of all on how far away you are. Off the tee on a par 5 hole, you could make your target be a generic line down the middle of the fairway—and hope for the best. But "hoping for the best" is rarely enough when it comes to hitting good drives. I am learning how important it is not to just kill it off the tee, not to say to myself, "I got a lotta room out there, so all I have to do is hit it as hard as I can, and I'll be fine." Committing to a specific target helps to restrain that impulse just enough to reduce the potential for your slice, snap hook, or sculled shot. Even if my target is a general area no more than 150 yards from the tee box, I want to keep that area firmly in my mind and make it as focused and small as possible. I will try to see it as the target during my practice swings. When I hit my drive, I try to be explosive but smooth, powerful but contained, dynamic but disciplined.

The target is as important a part of the process when driving as it is when chipping and putting. Without it, the drive lacks purpose; it has no *intention*. But the closer you get to the cup, the more specific and deliberate your choice of target becomes. Right now, the weakest part of my short game is determining where to land a chip shot so that it has a chance to roll toward the pin. In my earlier years of playing, I just figured "Aim for the flag." After many serious miscalculations, I began to work on the art of settling on a spot to aim for. It would be at some distance short of the flag, a spot that would give the ball a chance to do some traveling after landing on the green.

I remember one summer where that was just about the only thing I practiced, and the results were very satisfying. I'd go to the practice pitching green, throw ten balls out to various distances from one or another of the two flags and start pitching away. Of course, I can't do anything like this without inventing some sort of game or other, so the game was to count the total number of shots until all ten balls were in one or another of the cups. Then, I'd go back out and try to beat my score. Silly little game but talk about killing five birds or more with one stone: chipping from a distance, chipping from in close, bump-and-runs, putting from a distance, putting from in close, dealing with pressure and competition, learning how to put backspin on the ball, judging distances, and practicing the stiff-left-forearm strategy (see Chapter 3).

I'm not going make a speech here about the "practice makes perfect" routine, because any golfer who's even halfway serious about his or her game knows this, believes it, and does it. When I first started to play seriously, driving was about the only thing I practiced. It didn't take me long to figure out why putting greens, sand traps, and pitching greens are scattered around most clubhouses in addition to a driving range. Lately, I've been spending more time thinking about and practicing short-game shots and putting because these are the areas where my execution just doesn't reflect my intention.

Back to the second of the three commitments for a moment. When you putt, pick a very small spot and putt to it on the green. If there's a break (a slope) somewhere in your target line, try making an adjustment. That is, putt to a target point *off* the line between your ball and the cup. Professionals all have various strategies for this kind of putting work, so read up on it, take a lesson, or just watch some matches. If you don't like doing any of these, go out to the putting green at the club and start putting. The key is to commit to a target. That way you have a fair chance of being able to assess your outcome and to make adjustments if necessary. You need to test your commitment, in other words, and you would do well to test it before you are playing a serious round.

Deborah Graham's third commitment, committing to the type of shot, is the hardest one, and I will say the least about it because it's the one that will benefit the most from a lesson. Committing to the type of shot means determining for yourself what your swing must be. I hope that you have repeated this often enough so that it is familiar to you, a swing that resides in your muscle memory. Then, once you have begun your takeaway and gone all the way through the downswing, impact, and into the follow-through, you are committed to that particular swing. Second guessing yourself during your swing is very ill-advised. You'll know this immediately when and if you start doing it. Committing to the swing required by the type of shot you have committed to means that there are no hitches or switches once you have begun your swing.

After you learn how to do this, the beautiful shots start happening, and nothing gets you back onto the course for another round faster. After an errant shot, both my IPP and I have said that we felt our hands move during the swing, or we caught ourselves thinking during the swing, or we changed our minds during the swing, or something … when we both know that *nothing* should happen during the swing except the swing, and it's not *a* swing, by the way. If you commit to *the* swing, then it will usually be a good one. It will usually have good results, usually feel satisfying, and usually build your confidence for the next one.

Doing what we intend to do—executing—is a very complicated and unpredictable process, even in the best of circumstances. It's interesting to think about what the connection is between "commitment" and "execution." I don't think the latter is at all possible without the former. All I have to add is that doing a given shot correctly, even with a very affirmative and confident intention, requires having done a fair amount of physical preparation beforehand.

You can have all the best of intentions, but you have to give yourself the tools with which to carry them out. As soon as you have good clubs, good weather, a good frame of mind, some good practice habits, and you are in satisfactory shape and health, you should be ready when it comes to the execution part of this process. I'd say that all things being equal, the key factor in good execution is not allowing any distractions to enter your consciousness when you address the ball and take your shot.

That's why the pros step away from the ball when they hear some idiot click a camera. That's why a good golfer will wait until the plane has flown past overhead. That's why serious players don't like to hear people on the adjacent fairway making loud exclamations over good or bad shots. Execution requires all the focus and concentration you can muster. That's why detachment from everything that is going on around you or inside of you is absolutely necessary, and why a relaxed state of mind is so important in the process of repeatedly thinking to yourself, "intention and execution."

CHAPTER FOURTEEN
A RECIPE FOR CATCHING UP TO BOGEY

> Pile up enough tomorrows and
> you'll find you've collected
> nothing but a lot of empty
> yesterdays. I don't know about
> you, but I'd like to make today
> worth remembering.
>
> Professor Harold Hill,
> *The Music Man*

> If you can't laugh at yourself, then who
> can you laugh at?
>
> Tiger Woods

At one time or another during the four years of writing this book, every chapter has taken its turn as my favorite. I guess that means I've become comfortable with the entire book—or it might mean that the book as a whole is better than the sum if its parts. Perhaps it is just another sign of Attention Deficit Disorder which, as you might have guessed, plays no small role in the difficulty I have following my own advice on the golf course.

Speaking of which, think about this piece of advice given by Robert Preston to Shirley Jones as they flirt at the ice cream social in the 1962 film, *The Music Man.* Professor Harold Hill (Preston) says to Marian Peru (Jones), "I'd like to make today worth remembering." These words resonate as I look back over the number and variety of the suggestions offered in this book.

A Recipe for Catching Up to Bogey

Here are two dozen quick-hit reminders, instructional and inspirational highlights from the previous chapters that can make all of your golfing todays worth remembering, whether you're out on the course under a bright sun, in your living room putting across your living room rug into a jelly jar, or in the back yard chipping whiffle balls across the driveway into the flower pot on your neighbor's patio. And even if you're in the middle of winter, and the golf course seems millions of miles away, you can still make use of this list by taking another simple piece of advice from Professor Hill: "Think, boys, *think!*"

1. Keep your head down.
2. Keep your head still.
3. Keep your left (top) wrist locked in your short game.
4. Follow through.
5. Finish high.
6. Aim at the target.
7. Practice at home.
8. Take care of your clubs; make them your friends.
9. Hold your focus for a split second after you make contact.
10. Don't peek.
11. Stay on the fairway—OR—get back to the fairway as quickly as possible.
12. Safety first. Don't take unnecessary risks if it will cost you strokes.
13. Remember your "A-ha"! moments.

14. Positive thinking and putting have much in common.
15. Clear the mechanism before you start your swing.
16. Commit to the club.
17. Commit to the target.
18. Commit to the type of shot.
19. Don't expect miracles, but be open to their possibility.
20. Get your Inner Judge off the course; make him/her do the "Inner Judge Trudge."
21. Have an intention on each shot and execute it.
22. Don't sulk.
23. Keep your expectations realistic.
24. Look and listen to what's going on outside your game whenever you can.

I know what you're thinking now, especially if you're just starting out on your grand adventure as a bogey golf aspirant. You're thinking that this list is too much to keep in mind when you're playing. You're right. There is no way anyone can keep all of these items, or even just a few of them, in mind when you're playing a round of golf. You have to settle for working with one or two of them. If you play competitively, it could even be argued that you shouldn't keep any of them in mind, and instead, you should use the list for practicing or for playing by yourself.

Even if you are playing by yourself, however, the whole list is too much to think about in a single round. You should start out with just a few at a time, say in groups of three or four. You have probably noticed that some of them are specific technique-type reminders, and some are more general behavioral or attitudinal reminders. Select one from each type to work with, maybe two items per nine holes. The main idea is simple (remember Chapter 2): be mindful about your game in some form each time you play. Not obsessive, not preoccupied, not distractedly or distractingly attentive—but mindful. You need to define this word for yourself, and when you do, recognize that we are all capable of mindfulness to varying degrees. Embrace the trial-and-error method; use these twenty-four reminders in a way that works for you.

Here's how I would play nine holes with this list. First, to set the tone, I almost always remind myself that I want to stay positive. Then I'll define it further by telling myself that I will neither curse nor criticize myself. Then, looking at the list, I choose my pairs: numbers 1 and 2 as well as numbers 21 and 22. I do number 24 instinctively because I grew up in a bird watching family, so these are the five items from the list I will work on during my round today. I set my sights low enough so that I will not feel burdened, but I have set them high enough so that I will be challenged. If I play eighteen holes, I'll change my mini-list and focus on, for example, keeping the same ball in play, walking fast between shots, and numbers 16 through 19. The walking fast idea has three immediate benefits: it decreases the chances that my mind will get lazy, it "banks" extra time for me when I am setting up for a shot, and it's an excellent workout for someone my age.

I haven't said much about physical fitness so far, but I took up golf for several reasons, one of which has to do with the fact that at about age fifty-five, tennis gets noticeably more stressful on your knees, back, and wrists. I can still hit balls back and forth across the net, but I don't serve, change directions suddenly, or accelerate to chase down any hard-to-reach balls. Golf gives me exercise in a low impact way, but like any other sport, warming up and loosening up helps.

I can't expect my body to crank out golf shots, good or bad, without some sort of preparation. Flexibility is exceedingly significant when thinking about the role our *backs* play in our golf swings. If you have a bad back, for starters, you need to get into a regular exercise program, eat thoughtfully, and perhaps even take a muscle relaxant before you play. Yoga is another excellent way by which to prepare your body to withstand the mild stress of golf. Of course, your physician's advice must trump my advice without question.

I try to imagine playing this game when I am unable to walk eighteen or even nine holes. But, in fact, I just can't imagine it. I see young people playing round after round using golf carts, and I feel a sense of superiority. I like walking the course. It is one of the best reasons for playing. I walk fast whenever I can just to get my heart working, but I walk slowly once in a while to take in the day, the scenery on Lake Superior, or to check out the bluebirds, mallards, and ovenbirds that use the water and the woods of my home course as their habitat. I walk slowly when my IPP and I are deep in conversation. But I walk, and I will walk until they have to shovel me up with a front-end loader and carry me and my Strategy clubs off the course for good.

Last piece of advice in this recipe: believe in bogey and believe in yourself. The two will begin to feed off of one another before you know it. This is not rocket science, brain surgery, or professional golf. Start today and make today worth remembering.

CHAPTER FIFTEEN
EXPECTATIONS: FOREST AND TREES

Without going outside, you may
know the whole world.
Without looking through the window,
you may see the ways of heaven.
The farther you go, the less you know.

Thus the sage knows without traveling;
He sees without looking;
He works without doing.
                              Lao Tsu

Reverse every natural instinct and do
the opposite of what you are inclined
to do, and you will probably come
very close to having a perfect golf swing.
                              Ben Hogan

Back in the 70s, I lived in Durham, North Carolina, home
of Duke University, former home of the American Tobacco
Company, and during baseball season, the home of Tampa
Bay's Triple A affiliate, the Durham Bulls (of *Bull Durham*
fame). Believe it or not, I might have played one round of
golf the entire eighteen years I lived there. North Carolina,
no less: practically the Golf Capital of the World—if it wasn't
for basketball. Golf was a foreign language to me in North
Carolina: no rounds at Pinehurst, no watching the Greater
Greensboro Open (now the Wyndham Championship),
no vacation golf at Sunset Beach, and no visits to historic

Southern Pines. If I *had* played some of those courses a few times a year, maybe this book would never have been written.

I didn't know it at the time, but the work I was doing was becoming the cornerstone for this book. I spent twelve years learning about how to keep competitiveness in perspective at a quintessentially relevant Quaker institution, The Carolina Friends School, where I began teaching English in 1970. Quaker Meetings in Durham and Chapel Hill started the school in 1966 as an alternative to then-segregated schools in the Research Triangle Area. It was a powerful learning environment and remains so to this day. Learning is treated as a collaborative search for truth among faculty, parents, staff, and K-12 students who learn how to listen and respond to what Quakers refer to as "that of God in every person." The school community is tolerant, spiritual, and diverse.

I was not then, nor am I now a Quaker—but Quaker principles characterize much of what I believe about education to this day, and I absorbed a steady, inspiring diet of these principles every day at CFS. One of my colleagues at the school was Cal Geiger. He introduced me to the French-born Quaker, Stephen Grellet, whose powerful and inspiring words begin Chapter 5. Now an emeritus board member who still attends Friends Meeting in Durham regularly, Cal handled buildings and grounds work for the school in the 70s. This included maintenance, construction, trail clearing, remodeling, tree planting, road grading, and plowing from time to time in addition to being Faculty Elder. He also started the school's service learning program. Cal is a birthright Quaker, one of the most quietly devout people I have ever known. When he speaks up at Meeting for Worship, he occasionally tells a story that always concludes with the words, "Rest where you are." I try to keep that simple advice at the forefront of my daily activities, whether it's a round of golf, a classroom of students, or a punch list with too many items un-punched. It helps me maintain a kind of spiritual openness, and it defuses highly charged situations, inordinately high expectations, and the usual blizzard of daily obligations.

Every so often in those warm Tar Heel days, I'd see a bumper sticker that read simply, *"Expect a Miracle."* It was usually on the back of a certain Volkswagen beetle, and it seemed to me that the imperative revealed the little car's over achieving, very hopeful expression of wanting to be a Cadillac or a Mercedes; it would probably even have settled for being a Saab or a Volvo.

Reflecting on that saying, and pondering what miracle I might possibly have expected in those years surrounding the fall of Saigon, I think I was hoping that it might be any one of a number of possibilities: peace with honor in Vietnam, a cure for cancer, an end to Watergate, "our long national nightmare." Since Earth Day was enjoying a brilliant infancy in the early 70s, I considered that it was fair game just to expect a cleaner, safer planet. I began thinking that expectation was an interesting idea all by itself—apart from whatever message some foundation or advocacy group was trying to push with the bumper sticker. That was forty years ago, however, and back then I certainly hadn't done very much deep thinking about expectations—especially as they relate to the game of golf, much less bogey golf. Like many Baby Boomers in the 70s, I had come to have a rather complex relationship with expectations.

Most of us who emerged from the post-World War II period did so with a sense that our parents' generation had sacrificed a great deal for us—and indeed they had. By the late 50s and early 60s, we were primed and ready to put it to use. We took family, school, sports, and dating more or less seriously; we played hard and studied a little less hard, but at least we did well enough to get by—meaning we "got into the college of our choice" (or, in some cases, our parents' choice). We drank in the good times at the beach or the ski hill, at the drive-in or the sock hop, the ballpark, the company picnic, out in the neighbor's front yard playing whiffle ball. Though I can vaguely remember a few chums who added the golf course to that list, they were hardly a majority. Golf just wasn't that popular or compelling.

The number of Baby Boomers who are now playing on the PGA Champions Tour for senior golfers is small. The runaway money-winner, Hale Irwin, was born in 1945, the first year of this uniquely named twenty-year period, and the same year I was born. The only other notable Baby Boomers who have won more than ten million dollars on the PGA Tour are Tom Watson, Nick Price, Greg Norman, and Tom Kite: five golfers—total.

In our Boomer adolescence, we had been treated to an emerging stable of American sports heroes, thanks to Wheaties, the Breakfast of Champions, to trading cards from the Topps Company (see page 78), and a couple of fledgling weekly sports magazines. Curiously, these conduits to pro and college sports of every stripe still thrive in today's highly competitive sports marketplace, despite a blizzard of competitors. I had all three of them at my fingertips in 1954, but my golf acumen was defined by three names only: Sam Snead, Ben Hogan, and Patty Berg. I remember their images with unusual clarity, especially considering that my first love was baseball. I remember the pleasant smiles and the constant appearances in the headlines. Berg, who died in 2006, was a Minnesotan and still owns the record for most career major tournament wins at fifteen.

EXPECTATIONS: FOREST AND TREES

In those glorious halcyon days, reading *Sports Illustrated* ranked right up there with playing hockey on local ponds, watching the Green Bay Packers after church in the fall, and collecting baseball cards. The cover of the very first issue of *Sports Illustrated*, dated August 16, 1954, shows Milwaukee Braves third baseman, Eddie Matthews, swinging away in a night game against the New York Giants at County Stadium in Milwaukee. Inside the magazine are three pullout sheets of Topps 1954 baseball cards. The price of that issue was twenty-five cents.

Call me "old school," but I maintain that the magazine today is but a shadow of its former self; it's too clever by half, glitzy, filled with ads and quick-fix tidbits and quirky stats that have little to do with the overall quality of play or the drama of the games. For nearly four decades, though, *Sports Illustrated* gave us penetrating journalism, breathtaking photography of a pantheon of emerging or aging heroes, and nearly immediate coverage of most major sporting events throughout the year. The first issue is flat-out beautiful, but I am most fascinated by the second issue.

Of all the possible athletes, events, or scenes that could have graced the magazine's *second* cover, dated a week later, the editors chose a shot, uncharacteristically colorful for the 50s, of about a dozen golf bags all nestled together like runners at the start of a race. Golf! 1954! A full six years before the phrase, "Arnie's Army" was born. Mark Kauffman's photograph, used by permission as this book's cover, was prescient.

In 1958, the spring of my seventh grade year, Arnold Palmer won his first major, the twenty-second Masters Tournament at Augusta National Golf Club. He was one of the many sporting figures I kept seeing in fascinating color and reading about in legendary prose inside the pages of *Sports Illustrated*. One of

173

the magazine's legendary writers, Dan Jenkins, remembers 1960 as "… the year that Palmer, sweating, chain-smoking, driving balls through tree trunks, shirttail flying, took golf to the masses." Between 1960 and 1970, Palmer appeared on thirteen *Sports Illustrated* covers—third place all-time among professional golfers behind Jack Nicklaus's twenty-four and Tiger Woods' twenty-six.

It would be a reasonable guess that like many other Boomers, I took up golf just days after discovering Arnold Palmer in the pages of *Sports Illustrated*. However, though he influenced a generation of golfers, not to mention the game itself, I was not one of the converts. I was enrolled in tennis lessons by the time I was nine, so tennis had become my game. It wasn't so much that my parents preferred any of the tennis pros of that era to Palmer. I think it had more to do with the fact that tennis racquets were cheaper than golf clubs, and fewer accessories were required. Another consideration was that the tennis courts were closer than the golf course to our home, and we didn't have to pay greens fees or tip caddies. Ultimately, we had a tennis court built down in the hollow below our driveway which further distanced my three brothers and me from any thoughts of playing golf with our more well-heeled friends.

Luckily, I was no tennis snob, though, and I clearly remember the intensity my brothers and I summoned up whenever we played The Oak Tree Open in our yard. I would be Arnie (I was the oldest, so I got to call my player first; I was Arnie even when I played solo). We had a full nine-hole course, and with the exception of the pole under the purple martin house, the corner leg of our jungle gym, and a telephone pole at the south edge of our property, every hole was the trunk of an oak tree. Because of the size of the trunks, the odds of hitting a hole-in-one were quite favorable—if we remembered to keep our eyes on the ball and finish aiming at the target. That was not part of our skill set, though, so scores tended to be humbling—just like real golf. Half the course was on a hill, and more often than not, our downhill shots from the relatively flat second tee would miss the second oak which was just twenty yards downhill and still twenty feet up the slope from the driveway. Missing by an inch produced the same result as missing by a foot. The ball would bounce down the grassy slope, gather speed as it headed across the driveway, and roll down the bank out onto the tennis court. We always hoped our missed shots would have enough speed so that when they got to the tennis net, they would hit the taut netting and bound backward enough to give us room to make a decent recovery shot. We had to hit anywhere from a few to quite a few extra strokes to get back in bounds. To make things worse, it was almost impossible to "lay up" by getting the ball to come to rest *above* the oak giving us a sure two instead of a quadruple bogey or worse. I scarcely need to point out the fact that that hole was our number one handicap hole.

It must have been on this course that I started to learn about expectations, albeit at the subconscious level. We made the second hole a par 1 as much to encourage settling for bogey as to challenge us to hit the trunk on the fly in one shot. Lessons were gentle in those days, and they were remarkably plain. Most of the time, however, we just weren't smart enough to learn them quickly. One of my mother's favorite expressions, which my brothers and I assault each other with to this day, is the all too regrettable Dutch proverb, "we grow too soon old and too late smart." In retrospect, those carefree golf games in the yard would have made an easy transition to the real game if assorted other fascinations or obligations had not intervened.

The Vietnam War was counter intuitive to what my generation had grown up with. Following the Tet Offensive in early 1968, my young teaching colleagues, college classmates, high school buddies, and I learned that modifying our expectations would become not just advisable, but often a matter of life and death. The 60s careened to a close complete with assassinations, troop build-ups, acid rock, and protests of every sort cropping up across the country. We also learned how riveting the media coverage could be, and how endlessly fixated our generation would become on television coverage. Up until 1967, we more or less expected to graduate from high school, then college, and then either go on to grad school or get a job, maybe start teaching and coach a few sports, meet someone, settle down— "the whole nine yards." Those expectations vanished for virtually all of us in one way or another during 1968.

Thanks to the military draft and the lottery, we made some serious adjustments in our expectations. I was one of the lucky ones; I got a deferment first for teaching, and then for a bad knee. In the spring of my first year of teaching, though, my little bubble of American romantics in the morning, baseball practice in the afternoon, and Beatles music at night quickly became obsolete. I will never forget that year, not because it was my first as a teacher, not because I was finally in the work force, not because my very first apartment was in a "Make Love, Not War" Bohemian community in the conservative city of Wilmington, Delaware—but because quite a few of my students didn't care about sentence construction and Willa Cather. They wanted to know where I stood on Vietnam. They wanted support, advice, guidance, information, and most importantly, a perspective on war and peace that was *not* jaded, entrenched, safe, phony, or institutional—a perspective that I, in my leftover 50s state of mind, was entirely unprepared to provide.

Incongruous as it may seem to be talking about the 60s, teaching, and Arnold Palmer, I was working overtime to shape new expectations for myself at the same time as I was being besieged with the expectations of a whole new cast of characters. I was over-stimulated. I needed time to focus on what I was going to expect from myself in this brand new environment. I was fortunate to be working at a job where there were plenty of expectations to go around. I was unlucky enough to have to disappoint a few people who didn't think I should be listening to any other voices than theirs, much less shaping a voice of my own.

That's why to this day, I believe expectations remain a matter of "seeing through a glass darkly, but then face to face," both about ourselves and about the people with whom we live, work, and play golf. Check 1 Corinthians 13:12 to see the "glass darkly" reference. The New American Standard version changes it to "seeing through a mirror dimly," a translation that suggests that we must look at our reflection closely and carefully to truly know who we are, to see ourselves in the image that greets us on the surface. I look at myself much more realistically now than I ever did in those days because I have looked past the simple reflection of who I am, trying to penetrate beneath the surface. I try to take a more realistic approach to the whole process of "expectations," which means I have learned to treat my expectations on the golf course more carefully, to use them to best advantage, and to know at what level I will have to rein them in so that I don't self-destruct.

Our relationship with a world of high expectations is delicate, fragile, and unpredictable. I always used to think that high expectations are what lead to high performance. In many cases, that's true. College and pro sports, the military, heart surgery, high-stakes testing, NASA, entertainment law … you can make the same long list I can. All I can say about high expectations in golf is this: go ahead and have them, but make sure you have the necessary quantity of time, money, energy, talent, instruction, and solitude so that you can meet and surpass them without one or more wheels coming off the wagon. The most competitive athletes, the most decorated soldiers, the most gifted scholars, the most elite surgeons all fail from time to time—and *they've* spent their whole lives in pursuit of perfection in their fields. High expectations are not to be trifled with because with few exceptions the cost is high—as it should be. Above all, when and if such expectations enter our lives, we must make absolutely certain that they are our own.

Arnold Palmer represents a fairly large number of celebrities from that era who defined and embodied exceedingly high expectations for us. If you'll indulge me another short list, I'll demonstrate what I mean by naming one individual from several walks of life (other than athletics) from the pre-Vietnam Era:

Politics	John Kennedy
Classics	Edith Hamilton
Medicine	Jonas Salk
Music	Marian Anderson
Literature	Eudora Welty
Education	Neil Postman
Media	Marshall McLuhan
History	Barbara Tuchman
Science	James Watson
Archeology	Margaret Mead
Astronomy	Carl Sagan
Religion	Thomas Merton
Environment	Rachel Carson
Law	Thurgood Marshall

Certainly there are many individuals who could be substituted for each of these exemplary men and women. Whatever forces influenced the careers of these individuals, it's probably safe to say that they all learned how to deal with high expectations, those of others and ultimately their own, fairly early in their extraordinary lives.

But, after all is said and done, I want to deal only with "realistic" expectations.

I am trying to talk you into taking very seriously the making of realistic expectations on the golf course. If you do take it seriously, ironically enough, there's a better-than-even chance that your game will improve while you enjoy playing more. That's really the premise of the whole book, in fact. Making these realistic expectations will facilitate the following things (and this *is* my final list):

> 1. you will develop a comfortable margin for error;
> 2. you won't be difficult to play with;
> 3. you'll continue to see the forest as well as the trees (see below);
> 4. you'll earn more than just low scores and high praise;
> 5. you'll learn to take pleasure in meeting your own expectations;
> 6. you'll make and keep friends on the course;
> 7. you'll distinguish process from product more clearly;
> 8. you'll come to know the joy of golf's "inner game."

I have mentioned elsewhere in the book that once in a while during a round of golf, I invent silly expectations just for practice, such as no swearing, play with the same ball for the whole round, fewer than five (or three or two) three-putts, walk at a steady pace for the whole round, no trudging … something, anything, to concentrate on apart from the swing.

I don't always succeed. In fact, I hardly ever do, but since the cost is not very high, I don't have a sense of failure when the round is over. I say, "Well, maybe next time … ," "That was twice as good as the last time … ," or some suitably reassuring statement of closure. When it comes to the technical aspects of a golf swing, I know I'm not yet good enough to set unrealistic expectations for myself. I know that. I work hard on technical details, but I enjoy the game too much to let myself get excessively caught up in planes, angles, degrees, torque, and yardage. I know my limits, and I know what I need to do if at some point I decide that I want to push those limits.

I'll illustrate my point by referring to the 1965 film, *A Thousand Clowns* directed by Fred Coe. Martin Balsam plays a man named Arnold Burns, a hard working, relatively conservative, mostly routine-driven man. The main character in the film, however, is Arnold's brother, Murray, played by Jason Robards, Jr. in one of his first film roles. Murray is a flake. He can't hold a job, and he's not a particularly responsible parent or husband. He's a "square peg" who just keeps trying to fit into the round hole that is his life. Moreover, he tries to get his brother to do the same thing, and it's clear that that's not going to happen. Finally, Murray confronts Arnold and criticizes him for being boring and unimaginative, a slave to routine. Arnold replies, "Murray—I'm the *best* Arnold Burns I can be." Arnold Burns knows his limitations, and he knows his strengths. He is clear in his mind about who he is and what he can and cannot do. He has reached a comfort level that he has no further need of tweaking. Murray backs off and eventually he accepts the fact that he, too, must live and work with certain limitations on his own expectations in order to succeed.

Expectations: Forest and Trees

That's what I am encouraging you to do. Identify your comfort level. Develop modest expectations that will help you get there, not necessarily tomorrow, but some day. When you arrive, stay there and "rest where you are" while you experiment with new expectations. One summer I spent almost all my practice time with a wedge in my hands. Another summer, whenever I went to the driving range I would just hit my driver. Last summer, I didn't practice much at all; I just played. I have slowly figured out what works best for me to make small incrementally satisfying improvements in my game because I want to get to bogey golf. That, as I have stated and implied repeatedly, is my long-range goal: *relatively consistent bogey golf.*

The worst feeling in the world of casual or recreational golf is to *expect* a ball or a club or a shot to do a certain thing—and it doesn't. The expectation itself is not the problem; the problem is the complete letdown you feel when the expectation goes unrealized. If we dissect the process a bit, it might be possible to salvage the expectation part and retool the follow-up part. Here are three jobs to do:

> *Job 1:* Define the expectation specifically and realistically. ("I want to land the ball two or three feet from the green and let it bounce a couple times and roll somewhere, not sure where … I hope close enough to the hole, so I can one-putt at best, two-putt at worst.") Visualizing it before you address the ball is helpful. I want my mind to telegraph a believable and manageable picture to my body early in the process. Sometimes, if I can see where the ball is in relation to the green, and if there are no obvious complications, I start developing that image while I'm walking down

the fairway. I imagine this is what you (and millions of other golfers) already do. This is not a new idea, but I suggest it here because it is a *good* idea. Developing a little discipline where your expectations are concerned will add some order and some satisfaction to your game.

Job 2: Prepare to make that intention (see Chapter 13) take place. While holding onto the expectation, you go through your routine, whatever it is … three practice swings, a long look at the target, clearing your throat, hitching your sleeve, the waggle—whatever. At the point of address, you need to stop thinking about the expectation. ***Stop thinking about the expectation!*** It's time to let your body take over. Letting go of the expectation allows a much more relaxed swing, a more relaxed state of mind, a more instinctive and unconscious motion that you have rehearsed many times and imagined many more times. I occasionally admire someone on an adjacent fairway, and use the word *"effortless"* to describe his or her swing. That's the goal behind this second step: develop and practice a swing that is effortless.

Job 3: This step is actually the most important and, coincidentally, the most difficult. It's the follow-up talk you give to yourself. If things went well on the shot, you owe yourself some expression of satisfaction and praise. If things didn't go well, make sure you focus on why. If you get into an "I failed" or a "Why me?" frame of mind, or at the very worst, an (expletive deleted) mentality, there's not much hope for

that list of eight items above to fall into place
for you. If you have no idea at all why the shot
didn't at least roughly approximate what you
had envisioned, you have three immediate
options: 1) try it again, 2) prepare for the next
shot, or 3) shut it down, head home, and make
an appointment to take a lesson. You could also
spend half an hour on the driving range before
you leave.

I mentioned earlier that I felt that I didn't improve at all last
summer. That's not exactly true. I developed more confidence.
I hit more good shots. I learned how to be more exacting in my
putting. I started hitting fairway woods more confidently. I got
more comfortable with the humility that the game requires. I
got more comfortable with the cockiness it requires. I played
in the first two golf tournaments of my life. And I thought a
lot about this book. It was a hugely enjoyable summer, yet
my handicap remained in the low 20s. I worked diligently
on the *process* and let the *product* take care of itself. I felt
good about my game because I had worked hard on several
different components—but not all of them. I was careful not to
accelerate my expectations unreasonably, and I was better able
to see the forest rather than just the trees than at any time since
I started playing.

Seeing the Forest for the Trees

Suppose you ask me to write down in one sentence of twenty-
five words or fewer what I am trying to tell you in this book.
You also mention in passing that I can't use the "golf is a
metaphor for life" cliché. So I smile and shoot back that you
are just trying to save the cost of the book, and then I write
down your sentence:

Golf tests me as it gives me pleasure; it helps me understand my place in the cosmos and how well I respond to its challenges.

I could write such summary sentences quite a few times, and I'd probably include things like the sensory pleasure golf affords or the opportunity for deepening relationships with friends and family. I could focus on how much better I know myself since I started playing seriously. There are quite a few other things I could focus on, and I know that every golfer's twenty-five-word statement would be different.

In the meantime, for every golfer who just plays, there are probably ten who would mention that the challenges *on* the golf course translate really easily to the challenges *off* the golf course. In other words, golf *is* like life in many ways. You don't have to keep saying that to yourself. You don't have to make lists like I do, or keep a journal, or "process" every round you play with a reader or a listener, or by yourself.

What we must agree on (and golf is not unique in this by any means) is the fact that incorporating the game into our lives makes our lives richer—no matter what score we post or how many bogeys we shoot. That's the *"forest."* The *"trees"* are the countless rounds we play, balls we lose, shots we butcher, courses we visit, partners we play with, bodies of water we step in (on purpose or otherwise), scorecards we turn in or throw away, and beverages we buy from the drink cart girl. While you're at it, keep my old friend Cal Geiger's helpful phrase in mind: "Rest where you are." There is always so much more to see and hear in those trees if we are willing to listen.

Playing bogey golf is not just a lofty ambition; it can also become an expectation. Speaking for myself, when that expectation becomes my truth, it will be High Times. Writing this book has helped me crystallize that fact. Even better than making bogey golf my *own* truth, however, will be knowing that I have helped *you* clarify some of your own expectations, whether that involves playing bogey golf or not. There is time to get inspired by something out there on the course if you haven't already. Birds, balls, birdies, or bogies—it doesn't matter. Appreciate that you *can* play, each time you *do* play, and it won't be long before that appreciation will include both the challenge and the deep pleasure that playing golf represents—regardless of your score.

Listen. Visualize the end of *Casablanca* when Humphrey Bogart and Claude Rains amble across the tarmac as the airplane carrying Ingrid Bergman and Paul Muni to freedom disappears into the fog. Listen, and maybe you'll hear that unmistakable, confident voice as it says, "Louis, I think this is the beginning of a beautiful friendship."

Captain Renault and Rick Blaine begin their beautiful friendship at the end of *Casablanca*

You're only here for a short visit.
Don't hurry, don't worry. And be
sure to smell the flowers along
the way.
> Walter Hagen

I hit my first golf ball I
asked myself where have
I been? How'd I miss
this? I couldn't believe
it. I felt free. Truly free ...
I felt like the world was
open to me. Everything
and everybody.

> August Wilson,
> *Radio Golf*

In writing this book, I drove myself to shoot way better than
par, not to mention bogey. I make no apologies to myself or
to you, though, for spending countless hours on the driving
range and on the practice green (read "at the computer")
trying to make this book into the equivalent of a career round.
I recognized from the outset that you might not get it, that
the ideas might be too fringy, but it was the very least I could
have done to guarantee that you could hold two seemingly
opposing ideas in your mind.

This book's quintessential message, its fascination with
the concept of bogey, might suggest to you that I would be
satisfied to have it reach just a few people here and there,

to have its message be moderately intriguing, and to have its organization, style, and editing be simply adequate. It might further suggest that I'd be satisfied to have you strive for bogey when it suits you, but mostly resign yourself to playing without much concern for how far above par you score. That's the implicit paradox that confronts you when you read this book, so I must here reconcile the two apparently contradictory messages.

There is a lesson in this: given the fact that I have no idea whether or not you appreciate this book or what you think of the idea of treating bogey as a friend rather than a foe, I worked hard to maximize the chance that your response would be favorable. In doing so, I spent too much time tinkering and tweaking, asked too many people for help, obsessed too far into the night about how best to express my ideas and convictions, and dawdled too capriciously when it came to selecting images that would enhance the text. I also cut myself off from too many people, and I settled for too inconsistent an approach to household and professional obligations.

Might one then assume that golf is a sport which, even at its best and most relaxing, can be the epitome of misguided pursuit of elusive goals at the expense of responsibility and obligation, a sport that requires a degree of focus and preoccupation that is impossible for most of us humble working stiffs to achieve? If so, then I suppose the question most of us might ask is, "Why should I put myself through this ordeal when I know beforehand that the outcome will at best leave me unsatisfied and at worst drive me crazy?" The question might more simply be, "Why bother?"

The answer comes in the full acceptance of the fact that even when we try our hardest to be perfect, even when we work hard with every fiber of our being to achieve a goal, we will, in all likelihood, fall short of the mark. People fail all the time at things they care very much about, and that does not, in most cases, prevent them from continuing to try again. I have felt more like Sisyphus in writing this book than I ever imagined possible, much more than I do when I play golf. Nonetheless, I feel comfortable telling you that there is nobility in Sisyphus's tribulations that often escapes people who do not know his story. It makes for good reading—and good thinking, so if you are inclined to look him up and read his story, perhaps you'll reread this book with a new knowledge of and appreciation for chasing bogey.

I hope to see you out on a friendly fairway some day. I probably won't be the one rolling a boulder up the fairway, though. Look for me, instead, dawdling in the tee box and listening to bluebirds. I hope I have at least a faint resemblance to Dr. Henry Jekyll when we meet.

ACKNOWLEDGEMENTS

When one attempts to write his first book, it's critical to find the best editorial help available as a hedge against every conceivable literary offense under the sun. My friend Jim Smith, provided that service for me—and ever so much more. The manuscript's slow metamorphosis very much reminds me of the change a clumsy, land-locked caterpillar experiences. Jim's editorial expertise, though it is mere icing on the cake that is our friendship, has been instructional, inspired, and exhaustive.

Luckily, I discovered a publisher for this book in my own backyard. I owe the book's deft elegance to Cecilia Lieder, who was accessible and insightful throughout the journey, both as an advisor and a publisher. I am also deeply grateful for Amy Varsek's illuminating drawings, her professional cooperation, and her enthusiastic participation in this adventure.

There are few words sufficient to express the gratitude I feel for the contributions from my cousin Dorothy Weaver-Podell and my aunt, Charlotte Brown. It is difficult for relatives who see one another often as children to remain close later on in life. I am very thankful that our family bonds have only strengthened over the years.

My two brothers, John and Jim Fitzpatrick, certainly helped me with my swing, but they also gave me invaluable help on several of the book's central ideas. Though not a golfer himself, my brother Charlie was the first to convince me that if I ever wanted to be a writer, the process would be ever so much easier on a computer. Whatever success I have achieved with computers since 1988, I owe largely to his longsuffering tutelage.

I am indebted to my friends Ann Redelfs, Bill Dryborough, Kathy Siskar, and Bruce Clark for their editorial assistance. The book would not even have made it to the caterpillar stage without Jonny Conant's inspiration. I am also grateful to Diane Hilden, Lisa Olson, Peyton Berg, Betsy Larey, Ellie Schoenfeld, Gloria Kittelson, Paul Schintz, Joe Maiolo, Peter Clark, Pat Daugherty, and my trusty and thoughtful neighbor, Wes Harkins. I am especially grateful to Tom Osborn, and to his daughter, Gillian Osborn, for allowing me to rediscover George Morrison's painting. My thanks to the estate of George Morrison and Briand Morrison for permission to reproduce this painting.

I would never have developed any fondness for the game of golf, much less for writing a book about it, without the devoted friendship of Laird Davis. Forgetting, for the moment, the number of wasted shots he has had to witness or the number of scorecards he has had to correct, if it were not for him, I still wouldn't know that your sand wedge may not touch the sand before your bunker shot, nor that a golf bag may only contain fourteen clubs.

Photograph by Jeff Frey

Phil Fitzpatrick has published poetry and nonfiction, and holds a bachelor's degree from Harvard, a master's degree in English from Middlebury, and is completing a second master's in liberal studies at the University of Minnesota in Duluth. He has been an educator for more than forty years and currently teaches writing and literature at Mesabi Range Community and Technical College in Virginia, Minnesota. In addition to classroom teaching, he has guided canoe trips in the BWCA, taught state history for the Minnesota Historical Society, dug dinosaur bones for the Science Museum of Minnesota, operated a fork lift for 3M, and sold books for Lake Country Booksellers in White Bear Lake. Phil started playing golf seriously in the summer of 2001 and has chased bogey on eleven of Northeastern Minnesota's many scenic golf courses. "The best thing about practicing golf," he says, "is that unlike any other sport, you can practice it in your living room. In Northern Minnesota, that comes in handy!" He is working on a book of poems about walking in Duluth, where he lives, writes, gardens, and still chases bogey.